A CHILDHOOD IN HYPERBOREA

John Little

A land '... situated in the north ... inhabited by the Hyperboreans, who are called by that name because their home is beyond the point whence the north wind blows.'

Diodorus Siculus. C.60BC

Foreword

Most people live ordinary lives in which they accomplish no great things that shake the universe and the author of this piece is no exception to that rule. However by the fall of the dice and the chances of life I found myself living in a most extraordinary place at a rather extraordinary time - in the town of Thurso in the late 1950s and the early 1960s. Because they were my formative years and the experiences I had round the town were the first that I had in which I exercised any autonomy, they stayed in my mind, printed indelibly and with a clarity that is undimmed by more than half a century's passing.

This, then, is a memoir and all that is in it actually happened; the people in it are also real though for obvious reasons some names have been changed. Some events have been telescoped for narrative convenience but none of them are fictionalised. There are those whose memories are held in real affection and some whose names have not been changed because they are particularly respected. There are no fibs here and all is as it is remembered, and where there is opinion on anything then it is opinion and nothing else.

Yours, reader, may differ, and that is fine. If you see yourself in this book, or someone you know, or think you know; if you see your Grandma or Grandad or Mum or Dad, then reflect – it may not be them but a connection in your mind. Or it may indeed be them and the names have been changed to spare your feelings. Be that as it may, what is set down is the truth as the author remembers it, some of bad, some of good and much that is indifferent.

I have nothing to hide from these years - there are very few 5 to 11 year olds who would still think that they have things to hide when speaking over 50 years later, so if while reading you think me a coward at times, or a trickster, or a thief or a liar – well I was all those things at various points and do not blush to admit it. There is no reason that I can think of to not tell things as they were. If you think my teachers awful or barbaric for beating me and my classmates then I assure you that they were not. If you think anything of my parents then think that they were typical of their time. They were from the poorer parts of the north of England and they believed that if you spare the rod then you spoil the

2

child. When I eventually had to leave Thurso and go to secondary school in England, the greatest part of the culture shock was that the teachers did not hit you – it took a long time for me to adjust to that. The world and attitudes on worldly things have changed much since I went to school in the Far North. If I am setting these things down for any reason at all then it is to show this.

Ordinary people get brushed out of history and our tales and narratives of the past all too easily get ignored in stories of great men and occasionally women. That last is a particular injustice in human history, but how ordinary men and women, boys and girls, of the past lived is something we glimpse rarely because they did not think their stories worth writing down. This is true even of the very recent past because in the hum-drum routine of everyday life there seems to be little there that is worth writing about. In my case I discover in my head a dusty old chest full of little drawers, which may be opened and a memory pops out. Some of them pop out at three in the morning, inconvenient and reliant on my waking mind to set down. Others are as plain and fresh as the day they were made. Together I hope they make a picture of life, or at least my life, in a place of great and good people, of a special place, a remote place, at a boom time in its existence.

I do not propose to re-tell yet again the story of how Dounreay came to be built. There are books on that for those that care to read them. Briefly, to set things into context, the United Kingdom Atomic Energy Authority (UKAEA) decided that they were going to build an experimental fast breeder reactor of a revolutionary new type. All sorts of sites were considered for it and the favourite was somewhere on the West coast of Scotland. The Conservative MP for Caithness was a remarkable man called David Robertson and as his political career went on he became more and more pre-occupied with the affairs of his own constituency, eventually resigning from the Conservative party in protest that they were not doing enough to modernise roads in the Highlands. He did continue to support the Conservative party even when sitting as an Independent, but it was his intense lobbying that secured the new atomic plant for Caithness. There are many people who think it was placed there solely because it was in a remote area and the casualties in the event of an accident would be minimalised, but while this may have been a factor in deliberations, it was not the main

3

preoccupation of those planning the new plant. Robertson was concerned at the economic decline of his constituency and marked it as a major triumph that his pressure secured the experimental power station for Caithness. The truth of this is freely available to be seen in the Highland Archives and in the UK Parliamentary Archives.

Once the decision was taken, events poured rapidly into place and Dounreay was built and functioning in a very few years. Developments were fast and thousands of people flocked into the area-scientists, engineers, builders, welders, geniuses, plasterers and all that it took to support the cutting edge of the UK's drive to have a nuclear power capability matching that of the Russians or the Americans. I have heard Thurso described as the Los Alamos of the UK and Dounreay as its Manhattan project. The brains, the activity, the creativity and the élan that coalesced round the town turned it into a cornucopia of human innovation, of vigour, and it crackled with energy. I do not mean the sneering 'Aye – radiation' that came later as the achievements and pride were swept under the rug in the rows over the foolish treatment of nuclear waste that took place. What I refer to is the pioneer and cutting edge of raw energy in human minds that seemed to hover over the town, a penetrating and exciting miasma of aspiration and innovation that you could almost cut with a knife.

Ah well.
You have to have been there to know what I mean.

This is my story and it may be of interest to some; I certainly hope so. To my wife, Ruth, I owe a debt for her patient listening and correcting as I read to her what I had written each day. Also for her painstaking reading of my manuscript and correcting my English and my typos, to a degree which would make Lynne Truss run for cover. I also owe a debt, and quite a few drams I should think, to Michael Cowie, Thursonian, gentleman and scholar who also read, corrected, stimulated my memory, corroborated and generally encouraged my scribblings. Our experiences in some respects have not been dissimilar and I found his help more than just a little useful. Thanks must also go to Jane Storey, Gordon Little, Derek Little, Emma McGregor and Doreen Grant for help and encouragement, and to my ex-colleague, Sue Price, who read the whole thing, found that it kept her interested, and encouraged me to publish it. Gemma Grant's artistic eye for cover design was also very useful.

It is my hope that you, reader, find this book of interest and that it engages your attention profitably; this was my world. This was where I grew up. If you enjoy it then I am glad. If you do not, then here I stand – I can no other. But I don't do refunds……

John Little   November 2015

A New Home

Across a wild and flat land a frigid wind blew flurries of snow from above the north wind. In summer this was a plain covered in heather, bog, small pools, lochans, plagued with midges and uninterrupted by settlement. Its fringes were hilly, but scoured by Ice Age outflow, most of it was unremitting wilderness, without feature and hidden under a snowy and frozen blanket. If not hostile to human life it was at least indifferent to human survival; outside of the Arctic Circle, which in fact was not too far away, it would be hard to imagine a more inhospitable environment in the depths of winter. Fierce, raw and utterly ravishing in beauty, it was not a place of compromises.

Traversing the virgin white paper of this chilly waste may have been seen late in 1958, a four carriage train with a cloud of steam trailing from it, ambling determinedly along a single track line which wove its way between peaty frozen tarns and lochs. Its existence was probably due to the dedication of Victorian folk to the shooting of grouse more than to practical necessity, as its purpose unfolded in the wayside halts it came to occasionally where a small platform and a dirt road showed the way towards a remote shooting lodge somewhere out of sight over the horizon. The line had not been built for speed but for access; its survival was not on grounds of economy but of strategy, for it led to a place beyond the north wind where land became sea, where a short ferry trip arrived at the wartime station of the Royal Navy. Nineteenth century grouse-shooting had given way to twentieth century strategic asset.

The train usually took four hours from Inverness to the Far North, but on this occasion was taking far longer. Although the track had been cleared by a snow plough not long before, the wind occasionally built drifts deep enough for some snow to have to be shovelled from the track by a team of men riding behind the engine; much more and the line would have been impassable. The first carriage and the last two were empty, and the few passengers huddled in the second one from the engine. A cruel fate had decided that in addition to their difficult journey the people on board would have to travel on a train whose heating system had developed a fault. The compartments had thick ice on the windows and breath hung on the air whilst noses were cold and wet.

The second carriage, the buffet car, was not full but on the counter was a steaming urn, and the stewards prepared hot food on a small gas cooker. It did at least remove the chill from the air, and two children, huddled in their coats and blankets were just about warm enough. Their mother had opened their suitcases and wrapped them in anything she could use to insulate them against the biting and frozen atmosphere.

They were all tired as well they might be for they had been travelling for 24 hours on trains, sleeping as they could. They had no money for accommodation and the first bed they would sleep in would be when they reached the far north to join their father in the new house he had been allocated. To Gill, aged three, it was not too much of a bother for she was wrapped up in a sort of cocoon and had spent more time asleep than her mother and elder brother. Jon, aged five, was more problematic for he was very bored. The novelty of staring out of the window had long since worn off and he could not yet read so could not occupy himself in books. Nonetheless, though his mother's temper and nerves were obviously frayed, all was calm because she was strict. He knew he would get a hard slap if he stepped out of line, so he behaved himself, but such was his normal inclination anyway, not being a naturally unruly child.

The bright silvery tea urn puffed out clouds of steam and Jon heard the water inside it slosh about as the train once again came to a halt, seemingly in the middle of nowhere. He looked out of the window and saw that this time the cause of the halt was not snow, but red deer. A huge herd of them had decided to cross the track in front of the train, which came to a reluctant halt in a rather deep and narrow cutting. His interest was caught in a novel way as he looked out and up at the edge of the cutting, for a stag with very large antlers was at the rim and the boredom of the journey left him instantly. For the briefest snatch of time he looked into its eyes and it at him in a rather disinterested way. There was no communication in its eyes as they studied him, though he was frozen with delight at the encounter. Then in the most casual way imaginable it poised itself and leaped in the air, clear over the roof of the train. Jon did not know that red deer can leap 15 metres in one bound, and as high as 7, but the ease and grace of the feat caught him by surprise. His mouth fell open and he could only come out with a loud; 'Oooooer!'

The deer did not care as it landed on the other side of the cutting and ran away with the rest of the herd. He did not care either, that his mother, though startled by his exclamation, had not seen it and told him not to tell fibs. Mother seemed to think that he told fibs a lot, and had he not been used to it then he might have felt resentment, but Mother thought a lot of people told fibs. This was normal, but he knew the truth, while she did not. As usual when she called him a fibber, he just ignored it and did not protest – it did not pay. The fabric of life's memories is woven in this way.

A few miles from their destination the train stopped and divided. Most of it went on to the county capital to the east. Two carriages which they went into reluctantly for it was fridge-like, not the buffet, were attached to a dingy black engine known as the 'Thurso Flyer' which pulled them about seven miles into a large engine shed which was the most northerly station in Britain. Father was waiting on the platform, which was a great relief because they had not seen him for months since he had been working up here and they had stayed back down in England. He scooped a laughing Gill up into his arms because she was his little pet and kissed her, whilst his son got his head rubbed, then he picked up the suitcases and they walked out of the station. They had not many belongings, and no money for cabs so the family walked, crunching through cobbled snow and ice about half a mile to number 6, their new home.

The new house was very new indeed and had just been built and was very sparsely furnished. The government had decided that a new and experimental power station was to be built and that since the local town did not have enough houses for thousands of new residents, they must also be built. Almost a new town was bubbling into life as three and four bedroom semi-detached boxes were thrown up on three huge new estates that effectively doubled the size of the town and trebled the population. Jon, who had always shared a room, now found to his glee that he had a small one all to himself, facing the street and just above the front door. His bed was already made, a blue pattern rug set over an eiderdown and sheet turned down ready. There was one red and white checked pillow and none of the bedding matched but he did not care – it was his own room and it made him feel very important.

The house was not too warm when they arrived for it had no central heating. Father soon got a fire going in the front room where the fireplace was small and reluctant to light. He had a way of plaiting sheets of newspaper into shapes that would burn more easily, and when they appeared to falter he took a sheet of newspaper and held it across the fireplace as a 'damper' to encourage the fire to take hold of the kindling. The children watched carefully because they had seen him do this before in their old house down south, and sometimes the newspaper caught fire, and then things got rather exciting because Father would get angry and say naughty words and then they would laugh as he stuffed the burning paper into the fireplace trying not to burn his fingers. In the other rooms, if necessary, a convector would be placed, or a two bar electric fire, which were just about enough to temper the iron hold of frost in the room.

Mother was very pleased. She had a washing machine now and would no longer have to use a washtub and posser. Monday was still washing day, but now you put the clothes into a tub with an agitator and it washed the clothes for you. The clockwise then anti-clockwise turns of the three arm agitator inside the turquoise blue tub were hypnotic and the children liked to try to hold its fans to try to stop it – but never could. When the clothes had had enough, you turned a button and the water drained out. Then you took a hose and squirted water into the tub and agitated it until the rinse was done. Then you squeezed the water out of the clothes with an electric mangle, which was mounted above the tub. Jon was not happy though because he had liked the old mangle back in England which you had to turn by hand - big for his age he had liked to help turn the handle, which was a struggle, but very gratifying to see the result of his strength in the streams of water pouring out of the clothes and down the gutters back into the tub before they were hung up. There was a considerable degree of satisfaction to be had from this but Mother expected him to help by directing the hose and seeking out any remaining suds which needed washing away. If she was not feeling strong, she would hand him the wooden tongs so that he could reach into the tub and pull the wet washing out towards the mangle. The

9

washer was second-hand but Mother did not care. The problem was drying, because it was often cold and it rained a lot. It was difficult finding enough space inside the house and the single clothes-horse that they owned was always up near the fire and loaded with drying items.

Father sorted this problem by answering an advertisement from someone who was moving and selling a Flatley dryer. This was a large metal box about three feet high, which had heating elements inside at the bottom and wooden slats at the top. Clothes folded over the slats, the switch turned on, and the lid in place, the washing dried very quickly. There was an interesting and rather tasty side effect. Goods locally were very expensive, and bread prices were much higher than in England, so Mother decided it would be cheaper to bake her own. When she had mixed her dough in a large stoneware mixing-bowl, she would cover it with a clean tea-towel and put it in the Flatley to rise in the gentle heat, then bake the result which was excellent. Later she discovered that it was even more effective to cut and shape her dough into loaves and baps and then let them rise individually before baking. The bread was delicious and the children would hang around with expectant eyes for the risen rolls to be baked and then cooled from the oven. They would be slathered in thick yellow local butter from Orkney and jam and then they would eat - Gill could manage one, but Jon usually had two. At first he was not very fond of the butter because it tasted funny to him, rather like vomit. Accordingly his preference was for Stork margerine, though his Father put him off that a bit by telling him it had whale oil in it. He was big for his age and used a lot of energy in running about outside. Since the bread did not have the additives in it that modern mass-produced bread has, it went stale within a day or so. This did not much matter as bread puddings were common at the family table and 'pobbies', or stale bread crumbled up with sugar and warm milk was the usual breakfast for the children. Food was never wasted in this household.

In the shops there were two prices on everything, one written and the other unspoken. The price on the label was the incomer price, but all locals knew that they would be charged the local price which was verbal and which was considerably less. It is true that it cost more to have goods shipped up to this remote part of the country, but the 'Highland Premium' was not enough to explain prices that were often double for the newcomers what they were for locals. Some were even higher than that, and until Mother got to know and befriend some local shopkeepers she resorted to having some food sent from back home in England. She would telephone her brother from a phone box, for they could not afford a home phone, as few people could, and send a postal order, and several pounds of bacon, wrapped in newspaper would come up on the train, delivered by the railway parcel service electric float at a price still far below the local one. At first there was a kind of closed expression on the faces of the shopkeepers as they tried to maintain an even composure in the face of Mother's protests about the marked prices, but she, as a working class girl from northern England, did not go for their mark-ups. As the weeks went by she demanded local price – and usually got it. If she did not then she simply did not go to that shop again.

Certain goods were cheap for they were local but the children grew to hate mutton. The cheap cuts were very fatty and Mother bought a lot of it to make stews. Full of carrot, turnip, lumps of sheepy fat, and barley, they were very nourishing and no doubt good for growing children, but rows were had over eating fat, which was 'good for you'. Jon did not much care if it was good for him or not; being forced to eat fat by a determined parent with a hard hand is one thing, but the downside to such an arrangement when the coerced boy vomits onto the table are very plain. The fury and the resentment and blind helplessness of a child in such a situation is one likely to yield a dividend in emotional terms, but not one which is altogether desirable. Jon grew to be reserved and to hide his thoughts and feelings from his parents who had very definite views of their own and did not abide variance from them. After he was sick at the table though, he was allowed to eat the meat but leave the fat. A much safer and much more palatable dish was tatties and mince which both children loved, and could eat their fill of; this was always greeted with a lot of pleasure whereas the mutton stew brought groans.

Kale was plentiful too, and Orkney cheese, bouncy and tasty, was sold by the local butcher who was visited most days. In the window, among the chops and sausages and mince, were wax paper cartons with a bulls head on them labelled 'Beef Dripping' and Mother used to buy these and bring them home, melt the contents into a pan and make chips.

11

When she had finished the dripping would solidify in the pan and sit on top of the kitchen cupboard with the lid on, waiting for the next time the family had chips – which was often. Chips and egg were a favourite lunch, especially 'mouse chips', which had flaked cheese sprinkled on them. This was particularly pleasing to Gill who was going through feelings of affinity with small furry things, and loved the thought that mice would be after her chips if she did not eat them.

One meat there was that the children learned to like and this was venison; not that they could afford to buy it from the butcher. Father worked with a thin dark-faced, wiry man called Mungus who had a license to hunt deer, and at weekends he would go off into the Highland wilds to supplement his living with a rifle. He would butcher the carcasses himself in his garage and sell the meat to whoever wanted it, and at knock down prices. The venison was good, though Father had learned to be careful about buying bags of potatoes from him. A highlander, he could buy his potatoes at a good price from locals and sell them to incomers at a price still far below what the shops charged. However, Father bought a bag of 'fine' potatoes from him and discovered that they stopped a couple of inches down into the bag and that most of it was last years' spuds - soft and old. He was not amused and though he liked Mungus he tempered it with a commercial wariness after the potatoes incident which was a pity really because the family ate a lot of potatoes – every day, mostly in the form of mash which Father insisted on calling 'Pom'. When Jon asked him why he called it Pom he said it was because he had been in the army and that was what everyone called it. Fair enough.

Every time the children ate venison stew they thought of Mungus's dog, a black and white mongrel cross that they had taken to for his friendly licks on their hands and faces. It obeyed its master these days without question, for it had good reason to. One weekend Mungus took the dog out hunting and when it was time to come home, the dog did not wish to. When Mungus told it to get in to the car, it repeatedly ran off, upon which Mungus said; 'Please yourself you bugger', got in and drove off. The dog ran behind and Mungus drove for 10 miles before he stopped and let the exhausted dog into the car. An intelligent animal, when told to get in the car in future, it always did so.

Salmon also came occasionally, but Father thought that the least said about that, the better.

Much changed when Collett-McPherson's opened their store at Pennyland and it was the wonder of the age because it was a small supermarket soon known solely as 'Collets' or 'the Top Shop'. It made quite an impact because it was a new idea - there were many shops in town and Jon was familiar with most of them, because Mother shopped every day. There was no fridge in the house and indeed most people did not have one, so if you wanted fresh anything you shopped frequently. In shop after shop you went in and were attended to by an assistant behind the counter who served you with anything you asked for and you certainly did not help yourself to anything. It was a new concept for Mother and for the whole town. She soon got to know and respect Mr Collett in particular, for he was a most astute businessman and sensitive to the needs of his customers. Not for him the business of a local and an incomer price for he was fair minded and a man of humanity and acumen. Mr Collett was fond of children and used to chuck Gill under the chin when she came in, asking how she was and making her feel special. Of all the novelties that he had on his shelves the thing that the children took to most was golden berries. These were physalis berries from South Africa canned in syrup and they were delicious with condensed milk or cream. The cream was tinned double cream and Mother used to buy it for the berries and make Jon shake it so that when you opened the tin it was all mixed thick and nice cream. If you did not shake it then what came out was not so nice to look at or taste.

One day Gill was ill with a sore throat and would not eat anything. Mother asked if there was anything she would like to eat and she said 'Golden berries' and not having any, Mother went to Colletts as she was now calling the shop. Behind the counter was Mrs Collett and there were no golden berries in stock at which Mother expressed disappointment. Mrs Collett asked why Mother wanted them so particularly and Mother told her - Mrs Collett reached down under the counter and brought out one tin, saying; 'I was saving these for our dinner tonight, but if your princess wants golden berries then she can have them'. Surely there is a special heaven reserved for kind souls.

On another occasion Mother asked Mr Collett if he had any Suchard's chocolate, which she was fond of – he did not but said he would get it - and did, which was surely as fine a response to customer demand as may have ever been seen. It paid off in a respect between customer and shopkeeper rarely seen.

One day Jon was sent to buy a loaf of bread, half a pound of butter and a bag of sugar with some eggs, and was given a ten-shilling note to pay for it. He did not know his money well at this stage and Mother was surprised when he came back with the change that the girl on the till had given him, which was eight shillings and sixpence. Pennies were scarce in the house at that time but Mother did not hesitate; 'It's not your fault' she said, 'but she's given you far too much. I'll not cheat Mr Collett' and she set off up the road herself to give the money back to the correct amount. It was one of the greatest lessons in life she could have given her son and a sure indicator that good education is not always intentional. Pay your way and do not cheat your friends is surely a good and moral message for Sunday school, but that day Mother put it into practise with a man who always dealt fairly by her – and so she did by him.

All furniture had to be ordered and the usual waiting time for it to arrive was six weeks. Not surprisingly, many homes had second hand furniture bought locally - and Father made bookshelves, a book-case and picture frames himself. As for television, later the centre of the living room for so many homes, there was one in the street, and it was owned by a policeman and his wife. Happily they had a son who played out in the street infrequently. Jon soon made friends with him when the weather improved, and it became a weekly treat to go to David's house at 5.00 pm to watch the Lone Ranger on the BBC. He liked David a lot but he did not seem to come out into the street much.

Jon's family did have a radio - it was a small valve set in a home-made wooden box with blue plastic cloth stapled to it - Father had made the radio as part of his qualifications to be a radio and electronics engineer. They did not listen to it much, but it exercised a fascination on Jon who once found it outside in the garage and tried to make it work for an hour before Father came in and laughed telling him it had no battery in it. Although he felt foolish for not noticing it, his feeling improved when

14

told that Father thought he could get better reception and was going to take it apart and work on it. The radio sat in the garage and never worked again.

Nobody on the street could afford a house phone, though Mother's brother in England had one. This brother was of elevated status in the household because he was a builder, drove a Mercedes and seemed to have lots of money; he was a self-made man who had made it and therefore was admirable; there is no doubt that he was the children's favourite uncle, though it may be that his habit of slipping them each a ten bob note when they went to visit had something to do with that. Occasionally Mother used to go out to a phone box and ring him, but mostly she kept in touch with hand written letters, which were quite frequent because her sister-in-law sent her the local English paper wrapped in a brown card cylinder, with a letter inside, once every week

Father liked cars but at this time he did not have one - a situation that would not last much longer. Every morning he got up early and went out before the children got up to catch the Tilly bus, which was later called a Minibus. It took loads of workers out 12 miles or so to the power station outside town. This did not last too long though because as the work on the station progressed, it was necessary for Father to be 'on call' and the power station had him put on the list for a phone, which they paid for. It was not to be used for personal things, and so was not, but it meant that Father could be called out at any time of day and night - the dark green Tilly used to be sent for him at 2 and 3 in the morning sometimes. To Jon the Tilly bus was an object of import and interest because he saw it as a symbol of the grown-up world and longed to ride it out to the power station and back. This was perhaps curiosity about what was happening out there, but he never did get to see inside it in all his time in the north.

He knew, as did all the children on the estate, that big and important things were happening at the power station and Father sometimes talked about them at home. All their parent's friends also talked about it and there was present in the air all the time s low subdued excitement and an energy to the town that crackled on the air. Everybody somehow comprehended that something special was going on, something that certainly the incomers were proud of, something at the cutting edge –

15

and that there were a lot of very clever people around the town doing things. Father said one day that every third man you passed in the street in the town these days had a science degree or equivalent, which may or may not have been accurate, but gives a sense of the concentration of thought in the area.

As the year wore on and the days lengthened the children were allowed to play out more and more. If the days in winter were very short of daylight, having only six and a quarters hours between sunrise and sunset, in summer it was as much as 18 and a quarter. Although they were usually in bed by eight in the evening, as Mother saw that it was broad daylight at 10.00pm she allowed them to stay out longer in the street as long as she could see and hear them. They blossomed on fresh air and exercise and almost lived in the street. The weather was good a lot of the time through that first summer and it was a halcyon time of cowboys and Indians, with Gill always as an Indian, finding diamonds in some smashed glass in the gutter up the road, an expedition with hearts in mouths into the next road and out of sight of home, and 'it' an awful lot, chasing round maniacally. Calories were used in abundance and none of the children in the street were in any way obese.

Dr Giddis became a familiar figure in Jon's house soon after they had settled into their new home - and that is perhaps natural because he was the family doctor. He was relatively new to the town and had come to set up his surgery in answer to the growing need for another doctor as the town expanded and originally came from Aberdeenshire. The doctor called in once a week and Jon thought that this was a normal thing and his car being parked outside their house every Monday mid-morning should have been a cause for gossip on the estate, were it not for the fact that it was parked outside 'Aunty Joan's' house every Thursday mid-morning. There were other houses he parked outside on Tuesday, Wednesday and Friday mornings, for being a canny man, he had sussed out when the woman in that house did her baking. He and mother got on like a house on fire, partly due to her originally being a Gordon and he from Gordon country, but when they started chatting there was no stopping them, and Joan would come in to join in, and Mother went over to Joan's on Thursday. On his rounds every day the doctor knew where he could get a cup of tea from a pretty woman, a fresh cake or scone and a nice chat.

He was a very happily married man and his wife knew all about his elevenses, but eventually she contacted mother and all the other ladies and asked them to restrict it to tea for she was noticing that he was putting on a bit of girth round the middle. She agreed, laughing for she had noticed the same, and the doctor accepted this though was permitted by Mother to have half a scone whilst she had the other – and no jam!

At some point during 1961 Father had acquired a second hand television set from Mr Chadwick who ran a television shop in Princes Street. He used to bang this set a lot in frustration at the snowy black and white picture and Mr Chadwick came out a couple of times to adjust the aerial for him. Beyond doubt the favourite programme was Dr Finlay's Casebook, starring Bill Simpson as the eponymous doctor. It seemed to Jon that Dr Giddis bore a striking resemblance to Dr Finlay in his thin and chiselled features and his hawk-like nose and keen glance.

Dr Giddis had something else though, which Jon always noticed the moment he walked through the door. Dr Giddis was lit from within. That is to say that he radiated a kind of aura or light which led Jon later to wonder if the adults could see it because they never mentioned it, or was it just children who could? This is a thing seen rarely in life and probably only from particular types of people. Dr Giddis's light just told you that he was good; that he was a good doctor, that he could be trusted and that you were utterly safe in his care. If there are guardians set among us to keep us from harm then here was such a person and a great soul.

In the new estates, which seemed to be where he did most of his work, operating out of his surgery on Granville Terrace, he was held in very high respect. It was deserved.

Jon was lucky in that he did not actually need the services of the doctor very much, despite having frequent colds. These were not matters for medical attention. Father was different because soon after the family had settled in to their new home he came down with single pneumonia and was off work for a fortnight. During that time Dr Giddis came to see him every day just to keep an eye on him and administer antibiotics, which was how he became so familiar with the house.

Jon himself was hardly ever ill, being in a very rude good health, though he did get into trouble with Mother one night. He woke up in the middle of the night and felt sick - why he did not know, but vomited copiously onto his pillow. That made him feel a lot better and he was so sleepy so he turned the pillow over and went back to sleep. When Mother came to wake him in the morning she called him a filthy little beast and clouted his ear while throwing the window open to get rid of the stink. Then she made him take a bath and it was not even Sunday night.

Sunday night seemed to be bath night for everyone that Jon knew. Everybody bathed once a week whether they needed it or not, whilst Father and Mother and apparently most people around did not use deodorants, though Mother did use scented talc occasionally. It is true that people smelled and that adults had their own particular and individual smells but Jon just took that for granted. Father smelled of cigarettes, for although he was not a heavy smoker he did get through quite a few in a day – but then again so did Mother. It seemed to him that all adults smoked. Some people smelled rather badly, but Mother said that it was because they did not wash enough. Jon must always wash enough she said or he would get 'imp' and everyone would think him a dirty bugger who did not know what soap was. When he asked what imp was she told him that it was impetigo and you got it on your skin if you were a dirty bugger who did not wash.

The only medicine he needed to take that made any impression on him was that for his eyes but this was not to happen until after he had started school. He looked at himself one morning in the mirror and saw that his eyes were crusty and the rims were bright red but he thought that was a good look – red eyes were different and they did not itch too much. As he walked off to school, carefully avoiding the cracks in the pavement outside the Sweyn Road flats, for he did not wish to pee the bed, he hoped that his eyes would always stay red, but it was not to be. Mother was waiting for him at the school gate at the end of the day and she walked him home via the surgery where she had made an appointment. Then she swung round via town and Jon found that his eyelids were being held down and ointment squirted into them - he did not like it much but his eyes turned normal within a very few days.

If Jon was not in danger from not washing enough or from bad health, it was perhaps his bedside lamp that was the biggest danger he faced at this time in his life. He liked to chew things, and would nibble away at anything that he could leave teeth marks in. This included the twin core flex of the lamp by his bed. It was great fun to bite the two parts of the cable apart into two wires instead of one. As he was doing it once his teeth went 'bzzzz'. Any sensible child would have stopped immediately and indeed would not have been biting the cable in the first place but Jon was, truth to tell, a bit of a numpty. He liked the sensation of the 'bzzzz' on his teeth so he decided to do it again. His teeth went 'bzzzz' and something like a tiny flash happened though he was unclear as to where it was, and the lamp went off. Father was not happy because he was doing something downstairs and whatever machine he was using had also gone off. He had to go to the fuse board and fix it; Jon decided then, ever slow to learn, that he would stop biting the cable and that he would not tell Father what he had been doing. He never did either.

Outside the house a whole new settlement was forming and a whole new society. Like a cat let out to explore his new territory, Jon had a place to learn, scent marks to leave, and nine lives. Time to use them.

Atomicers

The new estates were, at first at any rate, insulated bubbles because there were no local people living on them. All the new houses were occupied by people who had come north specifically to work on the new and very experimental atomic power station. Many of them came from other parts of Scotland, but such was the range of expertise necessary for the new establishment to succeed that there were all sorts of people from all sorts of places living in the new houses which mushroomed up almost, it seemed to Jon, by the week.

The man next door, George, was English and he had a car. It did not work, but it was a very posh one, always covered with a tarpaulin and was a Jaguar. Not many of the houses had drives or garages because most people in the country could not drive – universal car ownership was not a thing that architects vectored into their estate planning yet. A very few houses had garages but they were rare and designed for employees of more senior rank. George used to wear a red beret all the time, and a pair of oil stained dungarees, and whenever the weather was fine he would have the bonnet of the Jaguar up and be fiddling with it. Jon never saw the car running though the engine was started once and a huge cloud of black smoke jetted out of the exhaust at the rear with a large bang, which was quite exciting. He was a bit wary of George because Father said he had been a 'red devil' in the war, and Jon did not know what that was but it sounded scary.

George had a wife, Olive, and a small baby who were never seen out much though Mother occasionally went in to have a chat with her. Olive was extremely beautiful and had been an air-hostess before she married. Jon thought she did not look very happy whenever he saw her and Mother said it was because it was so cold all the time. It is possible that she missed her previous job a lot for she did not seem to be an experienced housewife. On one of the few occasions that Mother saw her, she appeared at the back door of the house, which was really on the side facing her house, with some whole mackerel in a dish. Her husband had been down to the harbour and bought them fresh off the boat for tea, and had gone out for a drink. Olive was in tears because she did not know how to gut a fish and wanted so much to do as he wished for his dinner but did not know how to start. Mother was patient and showed her how to gut them, but when all was finished, had to cut the heads off. The lady from next door was very grateful to Mother but she said she could not possibly take them and cook them with the eyes still staring at her, even though Mother said she could tell when they were cooked when the eyes went white.

Father decided that it was time that the family had a pet so he bought a black Labrador dog, which he called Jock. Jon liked Jock and was getting quite attached to him, but Gill was very wary of the dog because she thought he would bite her. Nonetheless, she allowed herself to be sat on the side step of the house with Jon and photographed with Jock sitting panting in between them, and she even managed a smile. Mother was not fond of Jock because he was not yet house-trained and did the toilet on her kitchen floor; she was very house-proud. Jock's card was definitely marked the day she left a casserole on the kitchen surface with the lid on to cool, then went out to see a neighbour. When she came back Jock had eaten the entire contents of the casserole and then been violently sick all over the floor. Father promised that he would see about getting some dog training lessons - but it was fated never to happen.

Down the road about 100 yards away, just across Castlegreen Road, there was an unfenced playing field. Along this road one day came a huge flock of sheep being driven in from the farms just outside town to the livestock pens at the cattle market right beside the station. Mother was in the kitchen, the children were playing outside and Jock came to the front door. He saw the flock heading purposefully, expertly shepherded down the road, and took off like a rocket. Jon and Gill shouted for Mother who came running through, but it was too late. Jock hit the flock with the force of a stone thrown into a stream. They scattered in all directions right across the field and the shepherds and dogs could do nothing. Mother ran after Jock, for she was a young woman, shouting at him, but it took her ten minutes to catch him by the neck and drag him back to the house and lock him up. It took the shepherds ages to find all the sheep and they were not very happy. Then Father came home. Jock was never seen again and Jon cried because he liked Jock - but Father said that Jock liked sheep so he had sold him to a sheep farmer on the Orkney Islands. The feelings raised in the boy's head by this were not comfortable because somebody had said that Jock would be put to sleep by a vet for ever, so at least now he got to have a happy life on the islands which could be seen across the water every day. Sometimes the truth is better and when adults lie to children, even white lies, and then tell the truth years later, it does little for trust.

It was perhaps to make up for this that Father bought Jon a bike. He had never had one before, and was used to running behind some of his new friends, one of whom had a tricycle and another a scooter with a brake on it. The bike was red and fitted with stabilisers. It was his pride and joy and he was soon hurtling precariously up and down the road on it. This was not dangerous with so few cars on the roads, and the estate was the safest imaginable place to bring up children. People did not bother locking their doors at night – and even when they went out, for the crime rate was nil. The estate was full of young couples, who socialised with each other and most of them had children. The exceptions were Ron and Ivy from southern England who lived next door on the other side from George and Olive, who were middle aged, lovely and friendly. Jon and his bike did not wish to be parted and soon after he got it he rode it with Mother and Father down to Scrabster and back though his bottom was a wee bit sore when they returned through not being used to be on a saddle for such a time. Father took a picture of him on his bike right by the Thurso sign grinning like a loon astride his new steed. Gill had insisted on bringing her new possession, which was a small pram in which she swaddled up her favourite dolly with blinking eyes and thick blonde hair – and Snowball, a pure white teddy that was definitely female with bright blue glass eyes. Of all things, Gill loved Snowball the best and she and the bear were inseparable.

One day Father was working outside on the step at the back door and was actually mending shoes on a last. Evidently this caught the attention of a young woman walking up the street from town. She stopped to look at what Father was doing and he looked up and saw her. She was extremely beautiful with good cheekbones, and a graceful upright posture and her name was Margaret. She said; 'It's a lovely day.' Father looked at her and said;
'Yes – it certainly is.'
Then he said;
'Would you like to meet my wife?'

She smiled the most radiant of smiles it is possible to conceive so that the refulgence of it lit up the road, and said most emphatically; 'Oh, yes please!'

How Father, who did not give the slightest impression of being in any way intuitive, had known her wish would never be clear, but that was exactly what she wanted. She had recently moved from the south of Scotland into a house further up in the estate, into a place where the houses were still being built, there were no neighbours, and she knew absolutely noone; her husband was at work all day and she had spoken to hardly anyone since moving in. Jon had made an excursion up there and most of the buildings still had no doors and windows in them. Father went and got Mother from the house and she, being young as well, invited Margaret in for a cup of tea. They took to each other straight away and so began a lasting friendship, which transcended time, distance and all shifts of address and circumstance. Mother's best everyday friend was still Joan who lived next door but one, but Margaret was a person of grace and culture and elegance and was a particular friend; ultimately the relationship lasted life-long even though only in the letters of extreme age and the very occasional phone call.

Jon was particular friends with Jan and Mick who lived in the last house on the corner of the main road. Their Mother, Joan, and Jon's Mother were forever in and out of each other's houses for coffee and talk, talk, talk. Jan was older than Jon and already at primary school whilst Mick was small and cheeky, younger than Jon. Gill made friends with Susie, the same age as Jon, who lived opposite Jan and Mike. She had a brother Davie who was smaller than Jon, but friendly so they played in the street, in each other's gardens and sometimes went exploring the neighbouring streets. They did not go far though for up one side of the road you entered the territory of the dread Cadburys. Jon never set eyes on the Cadburys that he knew of but was warned by Jan in no uncertain terms that he must not go up there because the Cadburys were big and strong bullies who would beat him up. Once he did look up the road and about a quarter of a mile away he saw two heads above a wall but Jan said; 'The Cadburys!'

This was in such a tone that Jon turned and ran back to his front lawn as fast as his legs could carry him. It must be emphasised that he had no personal basis for this avoidance, but with good advice discretion is certainly the better part of valour.

Just up the road on another corner lived Tommy. Jon was not allowed to play with him but he did anyway because he liked Tommy. When he asked why he was not allowed to play with him Mother said he was a 'Catholic'. Jon did not know what that was, but played with Tommy when he could – he liked Tommy's dad too who was like a bigger version of Tommy but with a moustache.

Right up the road lived Chuck who was an endless fascination because he only had one eye. Jon asked him once why he only had one eye, and Chuck said that it had been knocked out by a boomerang in Australia. Seeing that Jon did not know what a boomerang was, Chuck brought his boomerang down to the playing field for Jon to see. Jon wondered why he had a boomerang if it had knocked his eye out, and was not very keen about trying it in case it knocked his eye out. He sometimes closed one eye and tried to run about seeing through the remaining one, but he could not really imagine getting along with only one. It was not very convenient and you must be careful not to fall over things. No matter how often and how hard he tried he could not make the boomerang come back like Chuck said it did when it knocked his eye out. Neither could Chuck, so Jon wondered if it was the boomerang that had done it after all. There are, after all, many things that can cause a person to only have one eye, but it must be admitted that having an eye knocked out by a boomerang is a far more romantic and interesting way than most to lose one.

Just across the playing field, bordering Sweyn Road, the men were building a playground. All the local children wanted to use it, but it was not ready yet. There was a long metal slide but the men had wrapped barbed wire round it so that noone could use it. Jon thought you could probably slide down it if you laid flat but Father said not to. He said that one boy had already tried it but that he had caught his willy on the wire and it had ripped it clean off. Jon thought that sounded very painful and he did not wish to have his ripped off so he stayed off the slide. The swings could be used though and Jon liked that so he went sometimes to the playground. There were some bigger boys who were often there and he was not too keen on them. They stood on the swing seats and went higher and higher and higher which Jon thought very daring. Two of them had a competition and as he watched they went up and up and up at a tremendous rate until one of them went clean over the top and completed a full circle swing. Jon's admiration knew no bounds and he thought he could never be that good. If you do not try something then you cannot fail, and if you are not good enough to do something then you would not succeed. Jon was already having caution bred into him and having been warned that those boys would break their necks he did not wish to break his, so took no risks. Later he might have a few swings on the way to and from school, but he had not yet started school so did not hang around the playground often. At any rate he did not have to because Mother and Father knew that Gill and Jon both liked the swing so they bought one for the back garden. It was really for Gill who took great delight in it, but for a time it made their garden the best place to be for all the children in the street and even when rusty from standing out in all weather the swing stayed popular whenever the weather was dry enough to use it.

Once Susie got out a dressing up box and had it out in the garden on a sunny afternoon and she and Mike and Jan and Davie, Gill and Jon grabbed what they wanted or could get and sat round talking in the sun on a blanket set up in Susie's garden. Jon never gave a serious thought to what he was dressed in, and neither did the other kids who all had absurd costumes on, but the green net tutu that he was sat in was to stick in his mind for all time. As they played and drank their squash and moved their toy cars Father looked over the gate and saw Jon in the tutu. He laughed and laughed but somehow it was not a pleasant laugh.

'I came to tell you it's teatime' he said
'But now I've got something else to do.'
He grabbed Jon and picked him up, patting the front of his trousers.
'What are you doing?' yelled Jon.
'Just checking it's still there' said Father 'You haven't lost it somewhere have you?'

Jon was mortified and fiery red – nothing of that sort had crossed his mind, but this, in front of his friends who were gaping at it. It's a funny thing gender; to Jon he was a boy and the tutu made no difference to that whatsoever. In Father's mind it was clearly something else, but

25

with what ease are children humiliated, made to feel silly and shamed. It may well be that he thought he was doing his son some sort of favour by reinforcing his masculinity, but such thoughts were far beyond Jon's level of sophistication. All he knew was that Father had shamed him in front of his pals – and for what? Bad things stick whilst good is washed away, and bad things scar you in your softest places; so easy to do and so hard to mend.

Jon wanted to ride his bike like a grown-up and pestered Father to let him try by taking the stabilisers off his bike. Father did not wish to but Jon was so persistent that eventually he got his spanners and removed the stabilisers. To Father's surprise Jon rode off quite happily as if he had been doing it for ages. Father went inside, happy, Jon rode about for a while feeling much more grown-up and in charge, then got off and played a bit. This involved being the Lone Ranger with Gill as Tonto and chasing some of the other kids and shooting them. Then he got on his bike again and rode up the street a few yards and stalled at the corner of St Peter's Rd, causing him to fall off, straight onto his face and flattened his nose, which burst and bled like a squashed tomato. Strangely enough it did not break, but it was the first time in his life that Jon had ever been really hurt and he learned to treat his bike with respect. Falling off soon became a rarity. The strangest thing of all was that although he had made a complete mess of his nose, which swelled up like a small red balloon, he did not cry. Perhaps it was the shock of it that removed the immediate pain, and by the time it began to hurt and throb, the time for crying was past. At any rate the pain did not last very long once the blood had been staunched with a clean handkerchief and washed away with salt water by Mother. The biggest problem he found was that it itched horribly and even though he scratched it in the most delicate way imaginable to relieve it, he could not get the itch to stop and it kept him awake for ages.

Another sort of relief was available occasionally in rumours that swept round among the children in the street. Jon's attention was much taken by a story which went round the estate that summer. There was a very nice man who worked at the power station whose wife had a cat. He did not like the cat and the cat did not like him. One afternoon he came home from work after a very long shift and laid down to have a sleep. It being a warm afternoon the window and the door were open and he slept flat on his back, snoring with his mouth open. Some time in the late afternoon his wife heard the most dreadful cry and a crash and ran into their bedroom wondering what was going on. She found the cat dead on the floor and her husband clawing at his mouth with soap and water at the bathroom sink. It appears that he had woken up to find the cat defecating in his open mouth and had reacted outside his usual civilised fashion. Jon often wondered in later years if they ever owned a cat again, but for certain the man's reputation for gentleness was now tempered with the knowledge that he was not to be crossed. Since the story could only have got out of the man's house if he or his wife had told it, the provenance is doubtful, but it is of value in demonstrating how reputations are made in a small community – or unmade.

That summer Mother acquired a second husband, though not one that caused any sort of jealousy in her first A small community of travellers had camped for the season down the road, and one old traveller woman was being a pest. She evidently had a theory that if you kept coming to a particular door, then eventually you would be paid in order to see the back of you. She appeared at the door of number 6 one morning asking Mother to buy lucky white heather. When Mother said no, the woman said she should be afraid that her house would be cursed but Mother, who was made of stern stuff, told her it was all nonsense and she wanted no heather. The woman came back in the afternoon and Jon answered the door, when she asked politely enough to see Mother, so he shouted for her. This happened again the following morning and then in the afternoon. Mother knew this would continue, and Father was at work when it happened. Then she saw David's father, Maurice, the 6ft 8ins policeman, going up the road and asked him in to explain the problem. As he was sitting in his uniform in the kitchen there was a knock at the door and Mother went to the door to see the woman there with her usual spiel for the sale of white heather. Mother smiled at her, having no pennies to spare for such, and said; 'Oh just wait – I'll have to ask my husband….Father!'

Maurice loomed hugely down the hall and looked down at the woman and intoned in his best Scots Guards bass, for such he had been; 'Is this woman bothering you dear?'
'Oh no boss – I'm not bothering anyone – oh no. I'll be off then.'

She left and Maurice laughed as he also left to go home.
'She'll no bother you again I'm thinking!' Mother thanked him and he strode off home. He had been sitting a few minutes when there was a knock at the door and he went to answer it. There was the old traveller woman selling white heather.
'Oh' she said; 'I thought you lived at number 6!'
'Ah' said Maurice; 'You've been bothering my twin brother with your white heather nonsense as well have you?'
'Oh no boss,' said the woman. 'No bother - I'll be off and I wilnae bother you nor your brother any more.' And nor did she.

Jon was displaying a rather cavalier attitude towards traffic and getting bold. Across the road at the T-junction was a GPO box, which he and his friends had taken to climbing onto and jumping off. Engaged in this pursuit one day Jon heard his Mother call and immediately jumped off the box and sprinted across the road without looking. The poor man on the pushbike had no chance of avoiding him and he ended up with his front bike wheel across Jon's back as the latter sprawled belly down on the road. Mother saw this from the front door where she was standing and Jon got a clipped ear, a sending to bed and another clipped ear from Father when he got home. In the lateness of the summer, towards the end of August Jon's short-lived possession of a bike came to an end, for much the same reason. Susie and Davie lived in a house raised slightly above the road. Their Father being attached to the scientific employees he had been given a house with a drive and a very slight slope led up to a garage. The children used to ride their bikes down this short slope at speed because it was fun. Riding a bike down it gave a momentary rush of excitement. Jon raced his bike down the slope and turned sideways, falling off the bike into the gutter - and it was a good job that the car had well-adjusted brakes. The inside wheel stopped six inches short of Jon's head. He did not think much of the incident, but his Mother and her friend Joan had seen it all out of Joan's window. Not only was the bike confiscated, but it was sold. He was not particularly happy about that but learned that as he grew older, he could more or less keep up with his friends by running – and before too long he could run like the wind.

In sight, across the playing field there was a large old house called 'View Firth'. It had been bought by the power station and set up as a social club for their employees. It had a bar and function rooms and those inclined could have a good time there with all sorts of events going on, with the occasional dance. Each year they organised a sports day for the children which was good fun. Never having tried to race in a sack before, even swift footed Jon did not do very well and kept on falling over. Gill and her friends were watching and thought it great fun but he wished to do no more. Nonetheless he had little choice and had to suffer his leg being tied to the right leg of another boy and to take part in the three legged race. Somehow he managed to avoid the wheelbarrow race, but then it was that Mother came upon her finest hour. All the Mothers had to line up in those full 50s dresses that they all wore, and solemnly place an egg on a spoon to race 100 yards to the tape. Mother's friend Joan led most of the way in a hard fought contest but 10 yards from the end her egg fell off her spoon. In a flurry of frock Mother raced ahead to win the egg and spoon race in front of all, flushed, triumphant and happy. It was for her a supreme moment, a triumph and a victory that was all hers; she had won and sometimes she needed to win - everybody does, occasionally. Of all places to be alive and to be living this was for her the best place on earth, now and always.

View Firth for the children was a place of fun because they always had a Christmas Party for the little ones and Jon still came into that category. It was splendid to be delivered to the door of the big house and ushered through into a great big room where there were cakes, and jelly and sandwiches and sweets. Then there was the funny man who did magic tricks and made them all laugh; then Father Christmas came in. Jon had never seen Father Christmas in person before, so the big booming man with the huge belly and snow-white beard who looked like Susie's dad, was an object of awe to him. Joining a queue to see the great man, when he finally got there Jon could only stare and sort of gasp a noise instead of a clear 'Thank you' when the real Santa handed him a present. He really wanted to ask if he would still come down the chimney on Christmas Eve - he had written a list and sent it up the chimney, and Father always put a drink and a mince pie by the fireplace for Santa before Jon and Gill went to bed. But he could not squeeze the question out - and it did not matter because he came anyway. Jon was allowed to open his present there and then, as were all the children in the room. It was a torch with a bullseye lens and four filters that you could turn. One was for normal torchlight but you could have red, blue and green as well and Jon was delighted with it, especially as it came with batteries and you could flash it across the field outside when they came out into the dark. The party eventually ended with all present sitting on the floor and looking into a camera for a black and white picture for the Power Station magazine. They all sat there looking at the lens, Jon, Gill, Susie, Mike, Davie, Jan and many others, looking agog, though Jon was smiling, frozen in time.

That was to come. For now the year was wearing on. The summer was closing down and September was coming. Jon had been five for a long time now and the time was coming, as it comes to all, when he would have to go to school. He was not looking forward to it.

Small School

When Jon woke that morning he did not wish to go. There is no doubt that he was not alone in this because after the long walk down the hill, by the playing field and down past the doctor's surgery, the playground of the West Public Infants School was full of children who also did not wish to go and you could tell by the quality of the noise which had much of keening protest to it. It was all right as long as the Mothers were there, but so strange. Through the forbidding green iron gates they went and into a yard thronged with boys. There were girls too but they were on the other side of a high iron railing fence and the squeals and cries on the other side were shriller if not louder. There was a sort of panic as Mother said that she would be back later, but for the first time in his life Jon found himself alone among a horde of others – and all more or less the same age as him. Some were tough and did not care, staring with bravado as the adults came out of the school to usher them into lines. Others seemed indifferent while others cried their eyes out and shouted for their mammies to come back in a furious and indignant way, pleading and demanding at the same time. Jon's eyes prickled but although tempted to howl like a lost boy, he managed with a furtive tear, to remain as if one of the indifferents.

He was never quick on the uptake and did not understand at first when the woman with the bell came out, that he was supposed to stand in line. That did not seem to bother her too much for she smiled in a friendly way and told him to join the line at the end. This was a comforting thing for she really seemed to be a very nice lady and he liked her look. This was just as well, because for the next year she was to be his teacher – the first he ever had. She was called Miss Bruce and had iron grey hair tied back in a severe bun. Formally dressed in a slim skirt and grey cardigan she looked rather like your stern granny but in reality she was one of the best friends her class ever had in their lives. They all trooped into her classroom and were told to sit on the floor by some friendly women whilst Miss Bruce went away for a few minutes. When she came back she had a line of girls with her, for boys and girls were taught together though they were not allowed to mix at breaks. Then she called out everyone's name and they had to answer 'Present'. Jon only knew this word in one context and that related to birthdays and Christmas. He got very worried indeed because if the teacher wanted a present he thought he would have to promise to bring one in tomorrow and he'd have to ask Mother to get one. To his great relief as the names went on it seemed that you did not have to say present, for some of the children said 'Here Miss' instead, so that is what he said.

It seemed that some of the children had an advantage because they knew their letters already but Jon did not. His parents took the view that this was the domain of the school. There were few books in his house and neither parent read much. Miss Bruce knew what she was doing and Jon spent his first day at school playing with plasticine and shaping it into letters and numbers, which Miss Bruce drew on the board. The moment that stuck in his head when the day was over was when he had to make two spheres of plasticine and stick them together. Then you had to poke holes through them with a pencil and make a figure 8. The exercise raised a conflict in him because the plasticine was new. It came out of boxes in lovely pastel colours and in ribbed strips, which were pleasing to the eye. It seemed such a shame to tear it apart and mould it into shapes that were not so pristine or pleasing, but eventually he did so.

Over the next few months Jon learned to read and write. The process was both inexorable and inevitable for Miss Bruce knew her craft – and she was kind. None could resist her kindness and she never punished – she was always firm. It is true that much of the learning was by rote, but it stuck and Jon's knowledge of his times tables up to 12 was to stay with him for the rest of his life. He turned six in the January of 1959 and within a short space of time was reading enough to make sense of the Beano and the Dandy. It did not strike him then, and did not until much later, that his reading at so early an age was any extraordinary thing for his classmates could all read and write with proficiency in a way that in later years struck him as a singular thing. Whatever Miss Bruce did with her classes there is no doubt that it was remarkably effective, and in his head there stuck a white stone in her memory as one of the best teachers he ever encountered in life.

Out in the yard you had to behave – the girls were over the other side of the fence doing their games and skipping, whilst in the boy's yard games of 'it' and football went on as in every school-yard across the breadth of the land. Round the back however it was a different story.

32

The pupil's toilets were not inside the building but tucked away in a corner of the yard to one side.   The entertainment at break and lunchtimes was rather more arcane in this place for here occurred the pissing contests. There was a wall separating the back area of the girls' yard from the boys' yard and you stood back from the wall to see who could piss furthest towards it.   It was that simple, save that the girls knew what was going on and found it funny, though they could hear and not see. Somebody had started the tradition of filling crisp packets with water and hurling them over the wall so that you could hear a chorus of female squealing when it exploded on the other side.   Hardly surprisingly the girls started to do it back - and it grew to be a game of who could dodge the water bags that the girls threw in revenge. The boys then figured that they had an advantage. They could piss into the bags so they stopped going to the taps. It took a very short while to realise that what was in the bags was not water any more – and then there were complaints. A member of staff was placed on duty round the back and the games were over. Dire punishments were threatened upon the heads of those filthy beasts who were guilty of the crime of throwing bags of pee over the wall…. Quite right too.

Effectively this destroyed the appeal of the back wall to the girl's area so the main yard became the favourite hangout for the boys and the back wall was deserted.

In the yard may sometimes have been seen a figure of dread - the Schoolie. The Schoolie was probably known to grown-ups by the title of 'truant officer' or some suchlike, but to the pupils he was a figure of awe and wonder. If you did not come to school or were late, so it was said, the Schoolie would hunt the town for you and drag you back to class, grippit by the neck. He stood by the gate clad in an old tan trench coat, hair slicked severely down to his head, moustache bristling, stood erect like the ex-solder he was, and exuding the air that you did not mess with him. As break ended he would set off on his rounds – and noone wanted to be on the Schoolie's round! Sometimes he was at the gate when school began at 9.00 am and the children gathered outside in all weathers waiting for the bell to signal them to line up. As they did so the girls would begin to chant a rhyme, which was apparently traditional and time honoured in this school, though where it came from none knew.

'What's the time?
Half past nine!
Hang your knickers on the line.
If you're late
Shut the gate!
And never mind your Auntie Kate!'

Who Auntie Kate was, nobody knew but the boys sang it as well and with great gusto, especially the knickers bit – but the gate did shut at half past nine and you were late after that.

At first Mother used to come to the school at 3.30pm to get Jon but that did not last long. He knew his way home and the town was safe so he was soon told that he could come home on his own and not to dawdle but come straight back. This he did for a while, but he was learning other things by now and had met other people and was developing ideas of his own. At the end of his first day he announced to his Mother that he had three new friends and their names were Grunt, Cue and Fillet. Grant, Hugh and Philip may never have known that their names were memorialised forever in Jon's head, but their immortality is assured as long as that lasts. Cue and Fillet vanished into a mental obscurity in Jon's memory but Grunt, whose face always became linked with that of Fred Astaire in its mischievous liveliness in Jon's head, was always a favourite with him though their friendship never developed beyond mutual regard. As the first friend he ever made independently in his life Grunt assumed a special place in Jon's head. Indeed it is with Grunt that Jon made a classic childhood error that should never happen.

As the year progressed the yard grew boring but the fence was porous if you were young and nimble. Jon and Grunt climbed the fence one day and went for a walk round the block. Noone ever knew because they were not gone long, just enough to taste the forbidden of being out when they were not supposed to be. Across the road was a church and George Street behind it had some bungalows, and in the front garden of these were snowberries. Easy it is to forget the temptation of forbidden fruit to children, though both Grunt and Jon knew they should not eat strange berries. Jon already had form on this, tasting the seedpods of a broom plant that grew like small peas against Joan's garden wall on his road, but they tasted foul. Snowberries looked much more tempting so they had one or two. They did not taste very nice and they had no more. Part of the reason for this was that Grunt said he thought they were poisonous. Jon had not really thought of that but he deferred to Grunt and thought also that they should not eat any more. In all justice they should have been ill, feeling sick and dozy and perhaps dizzy - happily to record neither of them suffered the slightest ill effects at all. Jon however had learned his lesson and benefitted from Grunt's advice – he never ate snowberries again.

What he did like about school particularly was the little break in the afternoon where everyone had to go into the cloakroom and Miss would hand out to every pupil a small bottle full of milk, which you had to drink. On each bottle the glass had letters saying '1 Gill'. Gill of course was Jon's sister, so at first he thought that the milk was supplied by someone called Gill, but learned soon enough that it was one quarter of a pint, though it looked more. Some kids had a small bottle of orange juice too, but when he asked if he could have one Jon was told you had to have a note from the doctor to have orange juice. Miss Gunn did slip him a bottle once that was spare, and it tasted funny – not like ordinary orange juice at all. It was nice but it had a sort of medicinal taste to it.

This milk thing was to continue right through little school and into bigger school and though he could not do it at first Jon soon learned a trick from the older boys. If you made your finger and thumb into an O and put the milk bottle top in there, and clapped your hands, the top would shoot up into the air with a loud 'Pop'. He could not do it for ages, probably because his hands were too small, but the day he managed to do it was a day of triumph and much popping.

Jon discovered a trait in himself just after he started school and was allowed to come home on his own. The route from school up Castle Street, into Granville Crescent and Sweyn Road was an unvaried diet and he preferred variety, nonetheless he obeyed instructions and went straight home to start with. However, his frequent shopping excursions with Mother had given him a good internal map of the local area, especially around the direction of town.

Her fondness for Rose's Lime Marmalade was to lead to a major step in his development for one day she gave him a two-shilling piece and told him to get a jar of it on his way home. There were no shops on his route so he had to deviate. The logical thing to do would have been to go up along Sweyn Road and head for Colletts shop but Jon was not going to do that. In Duncan Street, just below View Firth, was a small and not much frequented old-fashioned shop that sold bread, jam and a few other groceries and it was to this one that he headed. It was a good feeling, this exploring of places off his usual route and he liked the autonomy of it, though he could not have phrased it that way. He went into the shop and asked for the lime marmalade, and then he did something remarkable. There was a Soreen's malt loaf there on a glass shelf in the window, and Jon liked malt loaf, but he had no instructions to buy it. He took his first ever decision to purchase something, bought both items and took 2d change, then off home. It did not occur to him that Mother would be cross that he had spent more money than he should, and she was not. She laughed loudly and told him that he had done well because she liked malt loaf too. They had it for pudding that night smothered in good butter, not from Orkney.

Places have a smell all of their own and even school yards. The West Public had a schoolyard that was covered in ancient tarmac and ordinarily it did not smell at all. Ah, but when it rained it smelled; you could sense a tang of wet and moist old playground, larded by the playing of years and years of small boys and girls on its old surface. There was no smell like it anywhere else, and in all life you do not find it unless you are lucky and on the hills on the right sort of rock. When the sky grows grey and dull and a squall sweeps in towards you, if you are lucky then you may smell the rain. The smell of the rain; that was the smell of the yard, and it meant learning, tables, alphabets, prayers, hymns in the old church when the school had a special event in there, squealing girls, the Schoolie, and Miss Bruce. There are few places that have such an evocation and a perfume to them but the West Public had it – and still has it even now. Go and smell it if you dare smell the rain – and memories, the joys, and the tears of lost childhood.

Jon's stay at the West Public was not long. As the winter passed and the spring came in, the town re-organised its schools because of the huge numbers coming to live there and to go to school. Because of the

36

need to accommodate so many children, the West Public was no longer to house infants and primary children but only infants. Jon and his classmates were to move to the Miller Academy, which was now to be the primary school for the town whilst senior pupils went up the hill to the High School. Here children from the various infant schools in the district were to be melded into a new and quite large Primary School and taught much more formally than they had been. Even now the school was not big enough to take all the children so Jon found himself aged 6-7 in a hut classroom built just down the hill from the main building, bordering on the wall at the bottom of the school and with his second teacher Miss Veda Munro. Slim, elegant and very stylish she seemed almost out of place in her youth, for most of the ladies in the school were older women. Miss Munro dressed in slim-line black skirt, chic blouse and cardigan, short cut black hair and bright red lipstick inspired the most complete adoration in her boys and girls. Nobody messed her around – and especially not Jon who fell in love for the first time in his life, but he was not alone in this. Miss Munro cared. You could tell she cared by the flair with which she taught, by the way she talked to her pupils and by the way she carried herself. Modern and dedicated she did things that livened her lessons, making free use of the radio in her class to get her pupils going with the educational programmes. So when;

'A pussy went a walking and this is what he said – he said Meow, Meow, Meow, Meow – and this is what he said,' came thundering out of the loudspeaker everybody thundered right along without the slightest feeling of it being babyish or uncool. Boys and girls sang the roof off to this doggerel and as they grew older, to the strains of Bonnie Dundee.

The diet was varied and she often put on educational plays for children. Jon and his classmates followed with bated breath the tale of Wullie from Glasgow who had a big brother called Pat. Pat had been very naughty and was riding his bike without lights when a policeman caught him just as the episode ended. What happened to Pat thereafter Jon never knew because for some reason he never heard the next episode.

The tale of Peter and the Wolf by Benjamin Brittain narrated by 'his friend Peter Pears' did not go down with the class too well, but Kathleen Ferrier was unavoidable for Miss Munro loved Kathleen Ferrier, the contralto who had died a few years before. Her voice was a punctuation mark to the lessons, soaring, heavenly, rich and deep. Of culture they drank deep and were fortunate in their chatelain for in this house of learning Miss Munro was absolute ruler.

Jon did test her sense of humour to the limit one day, which came about through a trip to the dentist. Mother had a firm conviction in the benefits of munching raw carrots as they were good for your teeth and helped you to see in the dark – she said it so it must be so. One afternoon after he had got home and was hungry Mother gave him a raw peeled carrot to eat because it was not time for tea. Soon afterwards he developed a raging toothache and hardly slept that night. It was decided that instead of going to school Jon would have to go to the dentist with Mother. She was feeling sorry for him, and he was not happy with the idea of going to a dentist for he had never visited such a person in his life and Mother said that he would probably pull the aching tooth out. On the way down to the dentist, which was in Sinclair Street just outside the back door of the school, she told him that if he was brave then she would buy him a dictionary. He did not know what a dictionary was but it sounded a good idea and a special treat if he was going to win it for bravery, so brave he was and did not utter a squeak. It was not an adult tooth so came out easily, and when he had it out the dentist said 'Ah – what have we here?'

And underneath the tooth, in among the root of it was a small shred of raw carrot.

The dictionary was bought at a newsagent and bookshop just down the road near the Post Office, and very useful it proved to be. Miss Munro had decided that each member of her class would bring a new word in every day and read it out with its meaning, and this was how every day in class began. It was a very useful way of learning words, but lately Jon had been struggling to find new ones – or rather his parents had when he asked them. The dictionary made it much easier. Three days after he had acquired it the letter was H and the class did the round, each pupil providing a word commencing with H, and then it came to Jon who had found a word the day before which was really two words joined together with a hyphen, but the unusual structure of it and the sound of it appealed to him and he had chosen it for that. He now proudly stood up and called out his new H word ; 'Hanky-panky Miss!'

There was a pause in Heaven as if an angel had hiccupped – was that glint in her eye amusement? The heartbeat passed without perception as she said to the innocent, for so she saw he was;
'And what does that mean Jon?'
Reading from the dictionary he intoned;
'Trickery Miss.' and showed her the page.
'Yes' she said 'And a very good word indeed Jon - trickery it is. Now sit down please'.

It may be that some men, who cannot look after themselves in simple things, lose dignity in their inability to even sew on their own buttons. Miss Munro's boys and girls were not going to be among such inepts and one afternoon she produced a large box full of pieces of needlepoint canvas, large bodkin needles and thin coloured wools. Each pupil, male and female, had to choose two colours and the teacher then informed them that they were going to sew a table runner like this - and drew a chequered pattern on the board. She then demonstrated how to thread the needle, which all did eventually, and then to thread the wool into the canvas and loop it over five little squares and back on itself into the next row, and so on. When you had done five stitches you then missed five squares and started again with a gap in between. It was painstaking work and although he was all fingers and thumbs at first, Jon soon got into the swing of it, and although it took several lessons he ended up with a light blue and dark blue chequered table mat, though the edges left something to be desired. This was not a problem though for Miss Munro showed each pupil as they finished their mat, how to blanket stitch the edge into a border and make it complete. Jon was very pleased with the result and furthermore, had extrapolated the skill in his head to the point where he knew he could sew his own buttons on when they fell off, and from then on, always did so where necessary. Some of his fellow pupils had worked much harder than he had or were probably more skilful and finished their table runners long before he had – and Miss Munro had shown them how to knit; it is perhaps unfortunate that he never got that far; or maybe not since he was all fingers and thumbs and there – you can't be good at everything.

The lessons were not all practical though the pupils probably enjoyed those the most. In their year with Miss Munro they painted, cut Chinese lanterns, made plasticine models, paper chains of gummed strips at Christmas, sewed and drew. They also recited their tables a lot, sang the alphabet backwards and forwards and read out aloud. In January of 1960 Jon passed his seventh birthday and was by now a proficient reader. In fact he had been for quite some time and this was thanks to a company called DC Thompson who published two comics called the Beano and the Dandy which cost 3d each and which came out on two different days in the week. Mother did not give Jon money to go to school with, because she thought he was getting quite enough to eat. Some pupils did have pennies in their pockets and they were so lucky because into the school-yard, down the sloping drive every day there came a van selling sausage rolls, and buns and all sorts of goodies. Jon used to look at this with a kind of sniving envious feeling but there was nothing he could do about it. He used to have to run home for his lunch, and then back which meant that he was often late in the afternoon, but he used to hang round the crowd surrounding Big Davie from Spring Park who had a sausage roll every morning break. A nice and amiable chap, he used to occasionally give one of his pals a bite of his sausage roll, but it seemed a bit mean to Jon that he should be deprived of his food in this way. When school ended for the day Jon would run home up the hill and eat a doorstep sandwich of thick cut white bread, which he cut off the loaf, coated with margerine on each slice. What he put on it depended on how he felt. For a while he liked to cut slices of raw onion, then salt and vinegar them and eat that because Father, who was bald had told him that there was sulphur in the onion that was good for the hair. Jon did not wish to go bald, so had taken to raw onion in a big way. After his snack he would then run down to the station, as he ran everywhere, to get his comic.

In the station was a very small cubicle, which housed a newsagent who was a nice old lady with grey hair and glasses. Jon never knew her name because it would have been rude to ask it, but that is where he went to hand in his thick threepenny piece and to get his Beano or Dandy. She would smile at him gently and ask him how he was and he thought she was like a small bird that lived in a cosy house in the station, and he would never have dreamed of going anywhere else for his comic. The characters were such as he could identify with and admire in their cheek and their audacity, but his favourites were undoubtedly the Bash Street kids, for he knew them – or rather he knew people like them. He related mostly to Plug who was tall and ugly and a bit dim which is how Jon tended to see himself, but he did go through a phase of trying to emulate Wilfred by pulling his pullover up over his nose and talking through it. Dennis the Menace was a bit too brash really and Korky the Kat was not even human while Desperate Dan was a grown-up and a bit stupid. Minnie the Minx and Beryl the Peril in the Topper were girls but eventually the Beano was to release a character that Jon found most congenial to his taste and that was Billy Whizz who ran everywhere and was faster than anyone - that was Jon to a tee. As the years went by and he grew older he was to get more advanced comics like the Eagle, the Victor or the Valiant, but the Beano and the Dandy stayed with him late into his childhood. Strangely enough these comics were never discussed by the boys in his class – they were all far too grownup for that and preferred to talk about pop music because it seemed to be the fashion to know every new tune that came out every week – and there were so many of them doing the rounds that it made Jon's head spin. He could not be bothered with all that and stuck to the tunes that he liked, not bothering to keep up with those who apparently knew them all. Besides which most of them seemed to be about love and he had no time for all that nonsense.

Associating with other boys was having quite an effect on him by now; moving up to the far north and living at home for much of the first year had left his Englishness very much intact, but schools, as much as anything else, are melting pots. Now that he was at school Jon was mixing with other children who came from all over, from England, Wales, and Scotland. Living on the Atomic Housing scheme he particularly had not done much mixing with local children – but that now changed and it is hard to see how it could not have. Jon began to develop a slight Scots burr after a short time in the infants school, but the predominant influence on his speaking voice was not the flat precise English of Galloway, not the tuneful lilt of Eastern Scotland, nor the broad Gorbals patois of some of his new classmates, but that of the local population which is an accent all unto itself.

This was natural as the shopkeepers and other people that he came into contact with in his everyday life had the local tang, but now when Jon was talking to another boy he often prefaced his sentences with;

'Hey Bygie...' 'Hey Bygie – can I have some of that?'
Girls were 'Lascie'. Boys were 'Bygie'. At home of course he could not use it to Mother and Father but Gill was definitely a lascie.

He knew that the local area had its own way of life and culture, though perhaps that word or thought would not have meant much to him. Miss Munro was keen that her pupils should partake of all that their area had to offer and she was advanced in her thinking, wishing to show her class the great diversity of language. She taught them a poem.

E Lam Seil

E Lam seil dey hed coom et last
And at Geordag Sitherland's croft
E greit commoshun cood be heered
As they prepared fer off.

He ca'd e dowg a lazy cyard
A dode was Meery Anne
Twa stoopid eeshans were e loons
As roond e lams they ran. &c

This was a great thing to do because for some reason it removed a great pair of scales from Jon's eyes and made a link in his head almost overnight. You did not have to spell correctly in order to get sounds - they could come in other ways. He saw what he had not seen before, that long words are made up of short sounds and that if you link the sounds properly you get longer words and that there are reasonably logical ways to make those sounds, and that spelling and pronunciation, if you thought about them, were easy. Seeing the alternative in local dialect made it clear as crystal and must be marked with another white stone in the head as one of the greatest gifts a teacher can give a pupil.

As the year wore on and the weather improved, the green field of the Miller Academy, soaked for much of the winter, dried out and was

42

played on. It is odd that there were no organised games for Jon's class – they played no football but were encouraged out to run around all they could. A favourite occupation was piggyback fights. Being big and strong for his age he should have been the horse, but for some reason on this particular day Jon was the knight and the horse was not up to carrying him. As they struggled back and forward under the morning sun at break, his steed fell under his weight as he pulled the opposing pair off balance. They fell onto his right hand and it hurt when they went back into class.

Eventually it was hurting so much that he could not write and there was something wrong with the colour of it. So he put his hand up and called Miss Munro, showing her a little finger, which now looked like a small banana.

'Is your Mother at home Jon?'
When he said that Mother would be at home Miss Munro sent him to the office to get signed out and to go home.
'Tell your Mother to take you up to the hospital today.'
As he went out the door one of the other boys said;
'They'll cut it off - then you'll be better - they've got a machine that just takes it off - just like that!'
Jon did not like the sound of this one little bit but his finger was hurting a lot so off he went.

Mother took him walking to the Dunbar Hospital, which was not very far away from their house and the doctor looked at the sore finger.

'I think it's broken,' he said. 'We'll have to have a look at it. Wait here please.'

Mother and Jon waited and in his mind, with each passing moment there grew the knowledge that they were going to chop his finger off. Nurses passed. There was a strange smell of antiseptic everywhere. Jon determined that come what may, if they tried to chop his finger off then he was going to fight. Eventually the doctor came back and told them to follow him. They went into a small room, which contained a very big machine where he told Jon to put his hand onto a metal plate. He positioned the hand very carefully then began to manoeuvre the big

43

machine into place – to the seven year old mind it looked like some sort of gun. A vivid picture grew in Jon's head of a shining steel blade flashing down and removing his finger –' just like that!'

The doctor said;
'Hold very still!' and pressed a button. As he did so Jon yelled and snatched his hand back as fast as lightning and got ready to run out of the door.
'What on earth?' said the doctor.
'Ye're no chopping ma finger off!' shouted Jon.
'I'm not going to chop your finger off. It's a camera that photographs your finger so I can see if it's broken. Now put your hand back and hold still.'

The boy was not totally dumb – no blade had flashed from the machine so perhaps it was a camera - besides Mother was looking grim. He tentatively put his finger back onto the plate and winced slightly as the machine clicked.

Later, as they went home, finger now confirmed as fractured, and in a wooden splint, Mother was not happy;

'I thought I was going to drop through the floor with embarrassment. Don't you ever do anything that stupid again! Just wait till I tell your Father!'

She did tell Father. Nothing happened. Perhaps the broken finger was enough but having made an undoubted fool of himself he did feel stupid. You did not seem to have to explain things to children in those days, when they were supposed to do as they were told and it might have been different if someone had explained to him beforehand what was going to happen, but they didn't, such was the world and he was a fool.

That summer of 1960 school ended in July and the long summer holiday began. Jon did not know it but a phase had also ended. When he came back in September he would no longer be in the junior huts but up in the main building. Miss Munro, much regretted, would no longer be his

teacher. Life at school was about to be very different – and in some
ways horrifyingly so.

Big School

Jon ran, gasping for air, lungs and ribs aching, heart pounding, as fast as he could down Castlegreen road because he had woken up past the time and he knew what that meant. As he reached the top of the school drive, he heard a whistle and knew that he was too late. He was not too late for school, but too late for the line. When the bell went the pupils lined up outside their doors, boys outside theirs and girls outside theirs. When the whistle blew, they entered the building in silence and went to their classrooms where they mixed as usual. You had to be in line when that whistle went. Jon hurled himself down the drive and joined the end of the line but it would not do - and he was not alone. Waiting by the door was Mr Anderson. This was a man with thin sandy hair, keen eyes behind gold rimmed spectacles and wearing a long grey overall over his shirt, tie and jacket.

'Into the cloakroom,' he said.

That Jon would be late for registration because of this delay, because he had not been in line, when the whistle blew did not matter to Mr Anderson. There were nearly 30 boys aged 7- 10 in the green painted cloakroom, lined up with the backs of their legs to the form-benches down both sides, heads level with the coat pegs on the varnished wooden planking set horizontal to the walls.

'Hold out your hands,' said Mr Anderson, his spectacles glinting and each boy held out his left hand - never the right because that was the hand you wrote with, even the left handed people. As they held their hands out Mr Anderson passed down the line with a Lochgelly tawse and belted each hand in turn before saying 'Go' and the punished victim ran off to registration. Many of the boys were blubbing before he got to them but held their hands out straight. They knew that if they snatched their hand away then they would get two strokes instead of one. Jon had been here before; many times. He went home for lunch, and if late in the afternoon the same thing would happen. Since he was absolutely incorrigible and took a long time to learn, sometimes he had the belt twice a day, five days a week.

There was something else. He hated Mr Anderson and Mr Anderson wanted him to be on time so he was damned if he was going to do as the man wished. He tried to be on time, but it was not because of Mr Anderson. As the teacher approached him Jon retreated into that special place deep in his head where he could not be hurt. The tawse whacked down on the hand of the boy next to him and he cried with pain and ran off to his class weeping but Jon's face was a basilisk of indifference. The tawse came down with full force on his left hand and he didn't even feel it; he had ceased to do so months ago and no longer cared - it was just part of coming to school.

He ran up to the first floor and got into his classroom just as Mrs Gunn was calling the register. This was a kindly lady in middle age who was Jon's new form teacher for Miss Munro now had other charges and he missed her a lot. The new teacher was nice but somehow he felt he had lost something, though he did like Miss Gunn. Possibly he related to Miss Munro for her youth and vigour.
'Where have you been Jon?'
'Oh just getting the belt Miss.'
'Is that all?'
'Yes Miss.'
'Well go and sit down then.'

There must have been teachers in those days of corporal punishment who recognised that if you beat your pupils until it became normal, then it defeated itself because the sanction was no longer working. Mrs Gunn did not slap or belt ever and with all that was a very effective teacher.

Jon sat down at his desk which was old and metal and wood, smelling of age and etched with generations of carvings, initials, scribble and scuffs so that in some places the actual original surface did not exist but was made up of polish filled wood grain. At the front of the desk was a slit into where slates had fitted at one time but these were gone. Instead he picked up his pen, dipped it in the inkwell and began to write 'spelling test' in the general notebook he pulled out of his leather satchel. The inkwell was nearly empty but he knew this problem would be resolved in the next few minutes.

Sure enough the door opened within a couple of minutes and in walked a kilted figure carrying a large bottle of ink.

'Thank you Rory - go ahead,' said Miss Gunn and the boy in the kilt went from desk to desk with some degree of expertise and filled up each inkwell without spilling a drop. Jon was quite impressed because he thought that he would not be able to do it. He knew the ink monitor slightly but had not spoken to him much because he was an 'orrible and lived near the castle. That's what Mother said - he was the 'orrible Rory and that was apparently something of importance and the kilt was the sign of this, for it conferred an obvious status far above the merely short trousered mob that Jon was a member of. He also wore green wellies and was delivered to school by his Mother in a Landrover – and that all looked very stylish. The 'orrible Rory's father was a laird, which was why he was an 'orrible though Jon thought he seemed ok Mother said that Miss Swires, who appointed the ink monitor, only made him one because he was an 'orrible but Jon was not sure about that – Rory was so good at the job that it was probably talent.

Jon wanted a kilt badly because he had become a figure of fun in the school. Girls wore skirts and boys wore short trousers; there was no school uniform. All boys except Rory and his older brother who was too old to associate with Jon, but Jon was getting very tall and even lanky for his age. Short trousers began to look ridiculous on him and Father decided that he would have to start wearing long trousers. This caused a great deal of mental distress to Jon because he knew what the reaction would be – as the only boy in the entire school wearing long trousers, every eye would be on him and he would be a figure of fun. Could he not wear a kilt instead like Rory? 'No!' said Father so poor Jon found his free to the air legs encased in light grey and went to school with a sinking heart. He knew his fellows far better than Mother or Father did, and he was right. As he walked through the school gates he was surrounded by a hooting crowd, mostly of boys, but some girls too.
'Why're ye wearing trews bygie? You a' grown up now bygie?'
He could only reply 'Ma Dad med me!' but that only seemed to make things worse. One of the girls started to shout;
'Skinny malinky long-legs. Skinny malinky long legs', and they followed him round shouting it as the bell went to call them in.

At break time he expected more of the same and mooched outside miserably to lean in the sun against the outside wall of the school. Sure enough, smooth haired Michael was there being snide and a couple of girls sniggered, but to his surprise some of the bigger lads gathered round and said;
'Are they warm? Ah mean ye know – are your legs warm?'

He said that they were and then found that some of them had clearly been thinking. The air was cold and a wind was blowing up from the sea, across which could be seen the cold islands of the north. Some of them asked if they could feel the thickness of the cloth and somehow the mood turned to envy. The long trews not only looked more grownup and less childlike, but the good thick cloth meant that Jon was one of the few people whose legs were not looking blue with cold or goose-bumps. Within a couple of weeks you would have been hard put to spot a boy in the school still in short trousers.

The classroom in which Jon took most of his lessons was almost a hundred years old. The lower part of the wall was a wooden wainscot varnished darkly with age. The upper part was painted schoolroom green, though it could have done with another coat. There were cupboards on the wall painted a darker green in which books were kept, and on the tops of the cupboards were geometrical shapes – cones, cubes and cylinders and the like, all painted a dull dirty white.

Miss Gunn sometimes, but rarely, sat at the teacher's desk, which was raised up above the classroom on a dais. It was an unfortunate arrangement in some ways, designed 100 years before for ladies with elegant and very long skirts, the modern fashion meant that she preferred to sit at a table to one side. This was not always true of other teachers. Miss Swires for example, always on her dignity, usually sat at the dais, but if she lost her ladylike pose nobody dared to say anything because she was very free with the punishments.

In the big school pupils had most of their lesson still with one teacher. At different times of the day Miss Gunn would tell them variously to get out their spelling books, their English books, their Geography books, their Maths books and so on. But she did not teach everything. Miss

Swires taught handwriting, and Jon went to her for one hour a week on Friday afternoon last thing, so that was how his week ended. He dreaded the lessons but so did everyone that he knew. The handwriting lessons were conducted in absolute silence and this was maintained by pure fear. Miss Swires gave out copperplate stencils of metal, and ink pens and paper on which were lines to stencil letters onto. The stencilling had to be perfect and woe betide anyone who made a blot because the edge of a ruler would be brought down sharp on the knuckles of the offender. The situation was not helped by a story circulating among the children that a girl had offended Miss Swires so badly not long before that she had beat her so hard that her back was welted and bled through her dress. This may have been mere reputation for Jon had not seen it with his own eyes, but rumour is a powerful thing. One thing he did see that made him determine never to cross Miss Swires. A boy and a girl one afternoon had offended the lady and she made them sit on the dais in front of her. There she sat, knees tight together, glaring at the class, with two pupils in front of her facing the class. The boy shifted position; Miss Swires had told him to sit still and he had moved. As Jon watched she raised the heel of her shoe and dug it into the boy's back. Never ever cross Miss Swires.

One day however Miss Swires made a terrible mistake and crossed Mother. Mother had a fierce temper and once she had made up her mind on something she could not be diverted. One Friday afternoon in handwriting lessons he put his hand up and asked to go to the toilet. This was pure desperation because he knew well that Miss Swires would not let him; she did not let anyone go to the toilet. It is a strange and arbitrary thing that many teachers have in their heads that somehow nature can be channelled into man made slots, and that only wilful defiance can subvert their conforming to these times. Lunchtime was a long time before, and in the change of afternoon lessons there was not time to go to the toilet even if you needed it. Not for worlds would a child be late for Miss Swires' lessons. If Jon had needed to pee, it being halfway through the lesson, then he might have managed to wait, but it was not a pee, and he had already been struggling for a long while and needed to go. She would not let him and it was with a feeling of complete powerlessness that he part filled his trousers and waddled off home at the end of the day. In all fairness to him it must be said that he was by no means the first child to do this in Miss Swires' class.

50

He was in tears when he got home and told mother;

'I cacked my pants'.

He had never done such a thing before and that gave her pause for thought. She told him to take them off and go and clean himself up. As he did so she asked him why he had done it and why he had not gone to the toilet, and he told her. Mother was dark haired and dark eyed and sometimes had a gypsy look to her and this now showed as she raised herself up, eyes full of fire, shoved Jon's trousers and underpants into a bag and asked Joan next door but one to look after the kids because she had something to do. What happened next went round the estate because everyone who was left in the school building heard it. Mother went into Miss Swire's classroom and pulled out the soiled school clothes. She did not mince her words and told the teacher that her son had shit his trousers because she, Miss Swires, had not let him go to the toilet. Mother knew that there were other kids that had shit their trousers for the same reason, but now Miss Swires was looking at the mug that was going to have to clean it up. Mother stated that she did not approve of Miss Swires' policy and that if it happened again with her son, then she would bring the shitty pants down to school;
'And rub your bloody nose in them'.

Then she stormed out.

She did not tell Jon any of this – but he got to hear anyway, although not for a few days. Mother had been rather loud and many people had heard her. In the next handwriting lesson Jon performed as usual but wondered why the teacher came up to him twice in the lesson and asked him most solicitously;
'Do you want to go to the toilet Jon?'
'No thank you Miss Swires.'
He was careful after that to try to order his habits so that he did not need to leave the room after the humiliation of what had happened, but she always asked thereafter, which was nice.

Although organised games were foreign to this school at this time, Jon found that gym was fun for he had never been in one before now. He

51

learned to jump the horse, and vault the bar but he learned about the rope the hard way. Athletic and strong, when the teacher told the boys in their white vests and shorts to shin up the rope, he, who had never done it before, watched the other boys jump onto the rope and catch on with feet and legs. That was easy and he went up the rope to the top of the ceiling as if born to it. What happened next was entirely the fault of the Crimson Pirate although Burt Lancaster never knew of the utter disaster he caused in the far north of Scotland. Jon knew how to come down a rope – he had seen it done in the film, so he gripped the rope hard and slid down. He was about halfway down when most of the skin on his right hand and some on his left peeled off like a glove. The pain was appalling and the sting was unbelievable. They brought the first aid box but he would not allow them to put any ointment on it yelling 'No!' at them when they tried, so they wrapped it loosely in a bandage, and, as it was the end of the day he went home. Mother was having no nonsense. She bathed the hand and smothered it in antiseptic ointment. He could yell all he liked but if he did not shut up and get on with it then Father would do it when he got home – and you would not like that! For the next few days she changed the bandage and the ointment, bathing it in her sovereign remedy of salt water, and the fire of it was awful, though she told him it was for his own good. The hand crusted over behind the bandage and the young heal quickly so gradually new skin formed on the hands and eventually he could grip a pen enough to write again. All was back to normal in a couple of weeks, but next time he climbed a rope he came down hand over hand in the approved manner.

Death to the Crimson Pirate!

Mr Dunstable taught Art. He was young and intelligent, full of vim and vigour and all the pupils liked him and thought his lessons fun. You did not go too far though, because he had a particular trick with offenders that ensured that any who witnessed it did not wish to offend. Mr Dunstable was something of a painter and especially landscapes so many of the normal lessons were spent not sketching or colouring in or doing pencil drawings – but in actually painting on big sheets of creamy paper with brushes and water colours. Jon loved it, but one afternoon another lad decided to fool around and throw some paint across the room at a pal of his. This was a bad move. Mr Dunstable made a noise like a charging elephant and ran straight across at the offender and picked him up by the ears. Jon knew intellectually in later years that Mr Dunstable could not actually have picked him up by the ears, for he would have hanged him, but to his memory this is what happened. Presumably he put his hands up as Mr Dunstable's hands closed on his ears and grabbed the teacher's wrists to take his own weight, but it was obvious that the shock and pain was considerable. The teacher swung him out of his chair and dropped him on his feet in front of him, then he pushed him into a corner and yelled at him full volume;

'How dare you! How dare you behave like that in MY classroom you little animal! How dare you! Who the hell do you think you are?'

And so on until the weeping culprit could only stutter out;
'Sorry sir, sorry sir,' and was told to sit down, shut up and get on with his work. It was an object lesson in not messing round in Art yet perhaps strangely the class thought no more about it. Physical punishment was part of school and part of home. Jon knew well that if he was punished at school for something like what the boy had done, if he went home and told Father, then he would get slapped hard several times more for getting into trouble and shaming Father. All the boys and some of the girls knew this very well.

Jon was going through a pirate phase and had just finished reading his first full-length book, which Father had recommended to him, and bought down in the local bookshop - Treasure Island. Several of his art lessons were spent in painting a large half portrait of Long John Silver. You could not see his peg leg but his beard was rascally, his tricorne hat magnificent and the parrot colourful whilst in the background pirates buried a chest under a palm tree. Mr Dunstable praised it as a fine effort and stuck it on the wall for all to see. Triumph is a great thing – Jon liked Mr Dunstable and did not fear for his ears. Indeed he and some of his pals used to ask Mr Dunstable to pick them up by their ears – and he would oblige – provided that they had a good grip on his wrists first. That was a good laugh and made lessons fun. In Art it was clear that justice was served, the bad guys were punished and effort was rewarded.

He also liked Mrs Bain who taught music because her lessons were also fun. There was no false modesty about singing among the boys in his class - they all liked to belt out a good tune, especially a martial air. The music room was not a normal classroom but a sort of lecture theatre. Boys and girls entered and filed up steps into tiers of old desks like the ones in the classrooms until the people at the back were a considerable height above those at the front. Mrs Bain would then teach from her piano at the front.

'To the Lords of Convention, t'was Claverhouse spake
'Ere the Kings crown be down, there are crowns to be broke
So each cavalier who loves honour and me
Let him follow the bonnets o Bonnie Dundee!'

Jon had no idea what it was about but the tune was great, the sentiments fine and manly and his imagination was stirred so he sang it loud as they all did.

'Come cheer up me lads – 'tis to glory we steer
To add something more to this wonderful year
'Tis to honour we call you as free men
Not slaves
For who are so free as the sons of the waves?'

Mrs Bain chose her songs well though Jon and his male pals were not sure of some;

'My mother bids me bind my hair with bands of ruddy hue'
did not catch them in the same way for some reason.

The Skye boat song was fine, Rule Britannia was great, but it was when they began to learn John Peel that Jon contradicted his teacher and answered back. Mrs Bain played the tune to start the song, but she played the music for the second line of the song. Jon was a Cumbrian and Mother often sang the song at home. After a confused start he shot up his hand;

'Please Miss – that's the wrong tune'.
'Whatever do you mean Jon?'
'That's the second line Miss.'

There was a monetary pause and Mrs Bain adjusted her glasses and looked at her sheet of music.

'Why what was I thinking of? You are quite correct Jon. I am sorry! Well class let us start again with the correct music.'

Mrs Bain's mind was probably on something else, but her reaction made a great impression on Jon. A grownup had made a mistake, and instead of blowing up at him when he pointed it out, she had admitted it and corrected it. In life there are many grownups who are not capable of this as many children find all too well as they grow older, but to Mrs Bain there is no doubt that Jon owed two things; she fostered his love of singing, and she determined him that the best thing to do if you make a mistake is to own it, be responsible for it, and correct it. Mrs Bain was a grown-up - a proper one.

It is perhaps unjust that it was in Mrs Gunn's class late one afternoon that Jon did something that was to cause him lasting regret. History is not everyone's thing, though it was his. In the hour before end of school and during a lesson on Robert the Bruce, Ira was talking to his neighbour. Jon was listening to the story of Bruce and the spider, and was displaying a trait typical of him in that he hated interruption. Twice Mrs Gunn had to break off her narration and speak generally telling murmuring pupils to be quiet. Jon was getting irritated and he took a deliberate decision to get Ira into trouble, something that troubled his conscience forever.

It was some time beforehand that Jon had discovered a talent in himself for imitation and accents. He could bark, meow convincingly, and imitate people rather well. Now he put his head down and said; 'You bloody basturt.'

Strong stuff!

He said it quite clearly and distinctly and succeeded in making it appear to come almost from nowhere. But a thrill of achievement hit him when he realised that he had managed to speak in Ira's exact tone and timbre. A pause there was and then Mrs Gunn said in exasperated tone;
'Ira! How dare you use language like that in my class!'

55

This was a result. Ira was in trouble and Jon had achieved his aim. But then the laws of unintended consequence came into play. Mrs Gunn did not hit people but the next bit was not good.

'Go to Mr Anderson now and tell him what you just said'.
Ira's protests that he had said nothing were to no avail – she said that she knew his voice and he had to go. At any time Jon could have stopped it by owning up but now his triumph was replaced by shame and he cowered away. Ira took the long walk next door and told Mr Anderson what he was supposed to have said, protesting his innocence. Mr Anderson gave him the belt on his bottom six times. Jon, the despicable coward, was ashamed, glad it wasn't him, and said nothing. And learned the long lesson - that the burden of guilt is life-long and there is no remission of sentence.

Christmas was coming and in an old fashioned Scots primary school that meant celebration, but a certain sort of celebration soused in the tradition of Domini, scholasticism and the learned of the Manse.

Adeste fideles læti triumphantes,
Venite, venite in Bethlehem.
Natum videte Regem angelorum:
Venite adoremus (3×)
Dominum.

And so on. Jon knew 'O Come all ye faithful' well enough but the Miller Academy had views and thought that Latin was important. The carol was learned, all the verses, from the Latin text printed clearly and roundly on the board by Mrs Gunn, assisted by Mrs Bain, and the class sang it with gusto. It was understood that when they went to High School there would be Latin lessons so here was a good grounding.

It did not end there because Mrs Gunn wrote the word 'Jubilate' on the board and began to teach a song in Latin. Jon was not paying attention, but looking mazed out of the window in a far daydream. He missed the vital bit and then the class started to sing. There was utter astonishment in his mind as the class stared at the board and began to sing;

'You be lartay, you be lartay, you be lartay. Amen'.

The disconnect in his brain between the words and the singing was completely baffling and it took his mind several minutes of utter confusion before he again understood that letters are not necessarily pronounced in the way that they are in English. Eventually he got it, but it was never as popular in his mind as was the rousing Adeste Fideles, which he liked a lot, even in Latin.

It was in the history lessons though that Mrs Gunn excelled. Robert the Bruce has been mentioned but she gave a most excellent grounding to her class in Scottish History. King David fell over a cliff and that was a tragedy for it left Scotland without a King. The Black Douglas was a superman, capturing Roxburgh castle, attacking Carlisle and slaying the Red Comyn who was a dirty scoundrel who asked for it. At last Jon learned about Graham of Claverhouse and Killiecrankie, marveled over the generalship of Montrose, and wished that Bonnie Prince Charlie had had the guts to continue his march south from Derby. And of course Wallace, supposedly related to Jon's clan, and bravest of the brave, betrayed by the English and killed most cruelly. These were the bones of education in history.

There was English history too – William the Conqueror, Guy Fawkes and King Charles who got his head chopped off. These were enough to whet the appetite and to convince Jon that history was all about people and their stories; that it is downright interesting once you see that, and that in order to make it boring, you have to try very hard. That was powerful teaching.

A curious thing happened one day, which was unusual. There was a man around in the school with a camera, at least that is what the others in the class thought. It looked like a movie camera, but since Jon had never seen a movie camera he was not sure. Across the bottom of the driveway from the boy's entrance was an old house with a sign, which was called Mina Villa. Once a private residence it was used for some lessons for older pupils and seemed to be a fine old place, but since Jon was not supposed to go in there he never got further than the hallway before being told to leave. It was used partly by the Civil Defence organization and Jon saw a man outside there sometimes coming and going in a black uniform with a military style beret and wondered what they did there. The man with the movie camera if such it was, was outside Mina Villa and appeared to be filming the boys and girls leaping about the playground at morning break. Since he was standing right where Jon's group of friends met, if he did film them then he must have a movie of Jon himself and various other people somewhere. A thick crowd of boys and girls danced, swirled, ducked and dived all round the cameraman, and at one point Jon looked directly into it. Curious it is to have one's own image preserved for posterity in an ancient black and white film, and about as near to immortality as we may approach.

This was not the only occasion upon which Jon's presence at school was preserved for posterity, as was his haircut. In 1960 the school engaged a photographer to photograph all their classes. Each class had to line up in four rows – the front boys sitting, then girls sitting on forms, then girls standing on forms and behind them boys standing on forms. Jon had fancied his talents as a barber the week before and had cut Gill's hair quite short at the front before trying to do his own. Consequently his fringe was immortalized with a 30-degree angle between his left eyebrow and his right temple on the class photo. He stood in the middle of the back row, tallest in his class, squinting at the camera in a dark jumper with a white band across the top, and the collar of his white shirt peeping out. In the same line were his friends David, Michael, Grunt, David, Cue, Tommy, Fillet, Nick, Alasdair whilst in front of him Gillian, Dulcie, Hilary, Isobel, Helen, Christine, Tommy, Stephen, Jane et al, all squinting as much as him. The photographer had placed every class before the great front door of the school facing the full glare of the morning sun and each and every one of them squinted into the bright shining dazzle of a fresh morning, frozen like that for all time. Pupils in the future will see that students at the school in those days all had terrible squints…

Later, in 1962, the Miller Academy had its centenary so once again the entire school had its picture taken by class. They had the same photographer but he had evidently adapted his technique. This time the class was slanted away from the door and the sun was not in their faces. This time there were no squints, the smiles were broad and the nine year-old faces looked as happy as they probably felt to be out of a lesson and into the sun. Jon was not in the back row this time but 4th in from the left in a white windcheater, hair parted and with a decent cut this time. It had taken a long time for his angle to grow out.

Above Mina Villa but still in the playground area was a wooded hilly zone called Raven Hill. There were fights up on Raven Hill, worst during the autumn when bits of twig fell among the leaves and could be hurled at people. There were also places to hide and seek – and then there was the 'bike shed' to keep away from. This was a thick walled and concrete roofed building at the top of the hill beside the school gate, probably an old air raid shelter. It smelled of pee and you did not go near it – it was a big boy place and rumour said there was smoking in there though Jon never saw it. Ever willing to avoid violence, he never went in the shed, even to check out the truth of the rumour that there was a tunnel between it and Mina Villa.

1961 was the year of the 12th Caithness Music Festival when pupils from schools all over the county were invited to compete in a range of cultural contests involving writing, speech making and so on. Jon had a loud voice and Mrs Gunn had noticed it. She decided that he would be in the team representing the school, and although he did not have much say in the matter, he agreed to do it and to learn a poem off by heart which he would have to recite. On the day of the competition he had a very sore throat and a heavy cold but turned up at school to board the coach, which was to take their contingent to the County Town and off they went. Less than an hour later they arrived outside a large building, apparently made of corrugated iron and painted green and there they found boys, girls and their teachers from all over the county. It was quite a lot of fun to sit among so many strangers of his own age and watch them compete but Jon wished that his nose did not run so much and that his throat was not so sore. He was eight years old but the cold had done something to his voice and it sounded deeper than normal, and still loud, however much it hurt. Eventually it was his turn to speak as being in class 120 and number 19, and so he trotted onto the stage without any appearance of self-consciousness and really he had none - he liked to perform. Opening his mouth he began to declaim;

'Ducks' Ditty. By Kenneth Grahame.
All along the backwater
Through the rushes tall

Ducks are a dabbling
Up tails all…etc'

To his pleasure it was well received with a loud round of applause. At the end of the day he had to receive a little certificate giving his score. Overall he had come 8th in the county for his voice performance and received 85 marks out of 100, which was a distinction. You had to score 90 for honours.

The adjudicator had written on his certificate but he could not read it – Father interpreted it later.

'A very booming attack as the poem goes on. Voice sounded tired - don't rush your voice. You keep poem bright and cheerful. Diction crisp. On occasions you lose grip on consonants and the words just roll around your mouth.'

This pleased Father very much and he said,
'Just think – if only you hadn't had a cold and sore throat.'
By this time though, Jon had lost interest in the thing. His performance 'high' had worn off and all he wanted to do was take his cold to bed and sleep.

That the school provided a good education and a good overall experience for its pupils is not in doubt. They were, on the whole happy, hardy and they certainly learned a lot. All of Jon's classmates could read and write adequately and if you had asked him about 'special needs' you would have got a blank and questioning stare in return. The town and the school were going through turmoil as so many new people arrived and the success of its primary education in the Miller Academy was certainly down to Mr John Dallas the Head teacher whom most parents would have sworn an oath to his doing an excellent job. Mother certainly thought so, despite her run-in with Miss Swires. She respected Mr Dallas but wished he would not wear that long tan overall on top of his suit. Aunty Joan told her that if she worked in a school among all those dirty little oiks then she'd probably want to protect her clothes too, and Mother saw the point, but still thought he looked like the janitor and not the Head. Of the education he provided and of the school he ran, she had no doubts whatsoever; it was excellent.

Jon had no such thoughts as to the Headmaster's attire. He kept away from him for Mr Dallas had a reputation for being fair but strict and Jon had seen strict in action! One day in the yard the head teacher was on patrol among the crowds of kids playing, as he often did. His face looked to Jon careworn and slightly worried - there was a lot on his mind - but that mind was now elsewhere.

Society changed as Jon grew up and things began to happen that did not happen when he was in primary school, or very rarely. It happened on this day, as Mr Dallas did his round, that a boy lost his temper for whatever reason, and he hit a girl - slapped her on the head and the Head teacher saw it.

The mild mannered and quiet man that Jon had seen so many times, in his mind swelled up to three times his normal size as he crossed the gap between himself and the boy. His face betrayed a rage and anger that was frightening to look at, but it was mastered and controlled as he reached the offender. He grabbed him, not by the ear or arm but by the lapel and the culprit started to weep – he knew he had broken a taboo that few boys would then. He made no response as Mr Dallas said;

'Never. Ever. Hit a Girl. Never! Do you understand?'
The boy nodded miserably and the Head teacher said;
'My office', turned and strode off, followed without question. He got the belt on his bottom - how many times Jon did not know but he learned from what he saw. Never hit a girl - even Gill, and never cross Mr Dallas.

The people in charge of the Miller Academy were grown-ups and their students knew they were in charge; they were authority, the adult world, and they knew what they were doing. Their duty was to educate their charges and fit them to face the world, which they did very well. But school was also the place where you met people of your own age, and while you had to behave yourself inside the school perimeter, outside it was another matter entire.

Men About Town

Then there was Lennie whom Jon had met in school. Lennie was like the boy in the poem who had hair like knives and teeth like splinters. He became for a long while the punctuation to Jon's school life for they were best friends. Mother did not approve for Lennie was scruffy and badly dressed with few manners and Mother said that he did not have a very good home. She also said that she felt sorry for Lennie but did not want Jon to mix with him, which was fine because Jon had no intention of taking her advice. Lennie in a way seemed to rely on Jon's solidity and Jon liked Lennie's free spirit and fecklessness. A lot of the time he had a snotty nose, which he wiped freely and copiously on his sleeve, but this was the norm and much of the time it was cold and Jon's own nose ran a lot. Wiping noses on sleeves was more common than not among his classmates and was nothing to get upset about. Admittedly it was rather embarrassing when Lennie got invited to a party that Jon went to where there were loads of iced cup cakes. If Jon had seen what he was doing he might have told him that licking the icing off 30 cupcakes and putting them back on the plate was not going to make him very popular - but he did not, and Lennie did it. He liked the icing but not the sponge, which is natural and understandable but definitely not polite. Parties are polite.

For a while Jon and Lennie went everywhere together in the town and there was nowhere they would not go if they had the chance. It was with Lennie that Jon learned to be autonomous, because a companion arms you against all harm. When school ended Jon no longer went straight home but he and Lennie headed for the town to look and see. It was time to explore.

Down Sinclair Street there was a big green door, which had a sign for the Territorial Army outside. One day after school had ended Jon and Lennie wandered down that way. Someone had left the door ajar and Lennie looked in and said 'A tank!' It was not a tank in reality but some sort of armoured car with a gun mounted on top and there was ammunition in the rack – real shells. Wide eyed with excitement the boys decided to get up onto the car and see if the gun worked. They had just started to haul themselves up onto the car and climb the turret when a man in a uniform and beret came out of the back and saw them;

'Oy! What are you doing in here?'
Run like the wind and never be caught – both boys were fast and were not pursued.

They would poke their noses everywhere that they were not wanted. One day they nosed their way down Riverside Road and there was another door open where there was a sign outside saying 'Abattoir'. What it was they knew not neither cared. In they went and found themselves in a place where the dead bodies of animals hung from hooks on a rack suspended from the ceiling. On the wet stone floor were bits and pieces – long shiny intestines and a few stomachs lying casually about, blue grey and dead. Lennie looked at Jon - he had a queasy pained appearance. A stocky man in a white coat came out of a side office and saw them, but he was not cross at all.

'Hi lads – what're you doing in here?'
They told him they were just looking mister, and he saw that they were interested. 'Do you kill them yourself?'
Lennie asked with a wide-eyed morbidity.
'Aye - I do' said the man. 'Somebody has to or you'd have no meat on your plates.'
'Do you have a gun and bullets?' said Lennie.
Without speaking the man reached up onto a shelf and took down a squat black object.
'No bullets,' he said. 'It's a bolt gun. Straight into the brain - they don't feel a thing. Want to try it out?'

This last was said with a twinkle – the interview was evidently over.
'No thanks!' said the boys, Jon thinking that the man meant to try it out on his head, and off out the door; they heard a few chuckles behind them. Strange to say it did not put Jon off his dinner, or his meat generally, but it was a sobering experience that stayed with him as did the fact that the slaughterman was so nice to them.

Down on the harbour was a place that stank. Well actually the whole harbour stank because it was a place of work and a large number of drifter trawlers used it. Fish guts and scales were everywhere and there was no mistaking, even with a blindfold on, if you had such a thing about you, where in Thurso you were. The building that stank most was where they made the kippers and you could peer in and see rows and rows of kippers hanging there to smoke. Jon liked kippers and had them for tea sometimes because so did Mother and they were not expensive.

Nearby was something, which always caused the boys to laugh in the yard of old St Peter's Kirk, just the other side of the railings. There was a flat table grave on which was carved 'A Cow'. With no consciousness of irreverence or disrespect to the person buried there they thought it hilarious and speculated much on who might have buried a 'coo' in the churchyard and what colour the coo was. Was it a brown coo, a Highland coo, or a Frisian coo? And how long had it been there?

This would not detain them long because there was always the beach, skimming stones if the weather was calm, searching for razor shells and cowries which were prized because Mother had said that some countries had used them as money in the past. Round Thurso they were known as Groatie Buckies because somewhere near John o' Groats, 17 miles away, was a beach where you were supposed to be able to find a lot of them. Mother collected them to stick onto bottles, which she made into lamp bases and gave them to people.

In summer on the beach you could paddle, though nether boy could swim; there was no pool at the school and it was not on the curriculum. After a great blow out at sea you could find all sort of things washed up on Thurso beach though the biggest thing that Jon ever saw was a ship that had somehow washed up in the shelving rocks below the castle. It was not a big ship and it looked undamaged, though heeled over on one side showing its rusty bottom to the shore, completely out of the water. He wondered how on earth they would get it off but he never did find out. A few days later when he went to gawk at it, it was gone, and he assumed they had waited until the water came up with the tide then pulled it off.

Once tired of the beach you could go up onto Victoria Walk, through the caravan park and away home via Pennyland, or the Glebe up Holborn Avenue, or creep past the Police Station and go and look through the dingy panes of the red painted frame of the old bike shop window.

The reason for creeping past the Police station was again one of those urban myths that grew in the telling. Mother said that Jon must always behave near the police; they were walking down Sinclair Street one day when they passed an alleyway and Mother said that the police had taken a boy down there and beaten him up, so he had to be careful not to be cheeky to them. At the beginning of the alley there was a pale blue milk machine set back against a wall with three red buttons to select your drink. If you put in 6d you could choose a carton of ordinary milk, chocolate or strawberry. He liked the strawberry best and often put his 6d in the machine after school, but he always looked carefully before actually going into the alley in case there was a policeman on the other side of the machine. For some reason you had to be particularly careful of the Sergeant with the moustache. Jon did not know why but he was careful to go the other way if he saw this officer anywhere round. Maybe he thought he looked naturally guilty but he was far from the only boy of his age who felt this way.

The taste for the forbidden and the thrill of the chase soon became to Jon something to savour as he and Lennie ventured into the railway station, which was fine as it was not a busy place and had the old weighing machine to stand on and try your weight by sliding the bar over. The forbidden place was the Mart, which was right next to the station building where cattle and sheep would often be penned before being shipped off by train and there were notices strictly forbidding entry. The maze of grey metal pens fascinated the boys and they just had to explore. Occasionally there would be some beasts in the pens, bulls even, which was probably why you were not supposed to go near, but Jon like to scratch sheep between their ears and say hi to the bulls and just hang out there because it was diverting. It is true that there was a wee man there in an old brown pattern jacket and flat cap who shouted them and tried to chase them, but he stood no chance against two nimble footed lads who could hop pens like grasshoppers, excepting the day that Lennie slipped in the sheep poo and fell flat, getting up clarted in it. Jon found that hilarious though for some reason Lennie did not share his opinion.

Across the road was Ormlie Lodge, which was a big old house that had been extended and which was owned by the power station. It was apparently some sort of hostel in which they would house scientific staff, trainees, apprentices and so on. The garden was nice, and it was private and a place where small boys were not supposed to go. So Jon and Lennie did of course, and if it happened to be a hot summer's day there was a water tank on the side of the house with a tap where you could get a drink. What had actually sparked their interest in trespassing in this particular place was that a fellow explorer in school had told them that he used to drink at that tap and that once the men in the hostel had played a pleasant joke and emptied a bottle of orange squash into the tank. Alas Jon and Lennie were never so fortunate – water it was and water it stayed.

In Princes Street almost opposite the end of Paterson's Lane was a shop that sold sweets, crisps, chocolate bars and Wagon Wheels - a very large chocolate biscuit. Jon often went in there after school and liked the nice friendly man who ran It for Mother was quite friendly with him. But then he met Lennie and he also started to 'patronise' this shop but not for long. One day Lennie saw that the man's back was turned, he took a Wagon Wheel and went outside motioning Jon to do the same. Then he disappeared down the road. Jon handed a shilling to the man as he turned round and said 'I'm paying for ma pal as well'. The man had probably seen the whole thing in the mirror behind the counter, but there was a pause and he said gently;

'You can come in here any time you like son, but tell your pal he's not to come in here again.'

You had to watch Lennie because he would steal things and Jon did not – at least not yet.

Jon and Gill had a favourite shop, but this was probably something they had in common with most of the children in town. This was Jessie Allan's toy shop which was a cornucopia of all that could be desired. Although Jon's pocket money did not allow him to splash out in there he found the whole place a pantheon of delights and especially after he got a Triang electric train set for Christmas. Round the floor of the living room the black train ran, pulling a passenger compartment, an oil wagon, a flat wagon and a guards van. If he saved then he could afford a few more pieces of track from Jessie's, and bought them. To go with the track were several die-cast cars that used to get stuck crossing the tracks regularly, with no mind to being future collector's pieces, Dinky, Corgi and cheap plastic from Hong Kong were all subject to great disasters, even model planes crashing onto them from a great height. Gill being a lascie preferred the upstairs room in Jessie Allan's where were the toy prams and dollies. Boring! Why bother with them when you could buy a cap pistol with unlimited firepower, strap a holster to your waist, the laces round your right leg and just shoot all the other kids round the neighbourhood? Much more fun! That the gun was bright shiny chrome, and in no way realistic, did not bother Jon a whit.

Despite the thieving and the snotty nose, the scruffy clothes and the parental disapproval Jon and Lennie were inseparable for several months. When the end of it came, it was with a certain drama that drew a definite line to their relationship, and it fell about because of the boats.

Down on the flat area by the river, just upstream from the town bridge were two ponds. One was tidal and drained every low tide to be a large muddy pit, but upstream of this was the mill-pond which functioned as a boating lake. Beside it was a hut where reigned a man known solely to the local kids as Peter. Here for just 6d you could hire a rowing boat for an hour and great fun was to be had. You could race and splash or just lie in your boat, chill out, call to your friends on the shore, see how many times you could make it round the pond in an hour and generally just enjoy mucking about in boats.

One day in school, during morning break. Lennie did not feel like going to the next lesson, which was Maths so he said;

'Let's go and get a couple of boats and come back later.'

Jon thought that was a very good idea so he agreed and they went down the bottom of the field, hopped onto the school wall and jumped down into Janet Street. From there they took their time and sauntered down to the bridge, crossed it and then up to the boating pond. It was closed and Peter was not there. It seemed that there would be no boating today, especially as all the boats were tied up out at one of the islands.

Lennie was not bothered;
'It's no all that deep,' he said and jumped into the pond.

It was actually not deep. Jon did not want to get his shoes and socks wet so after telling Lennie, whilst laughing like a loon, that he was 'A mad Bygie' he watched as Lennie waded out to the island and came back pulling two boats behind him. They had a great time for over an hour, then they realised that if they did not get going then they would be late for afternoon register. Lennie put the boats back where they had been and by dint of hard running they made the line in time and went in, upstairs and to the classroom where Mrs Gunn was sitting at her desk. Beside her was mother and Jon's jaw just about hit the floor. It may be gathered that he was not then, as ever, quick on the uptake, though he did learn lessons well by repetition. If he and Lennie had troubled to think of it then they might have looked out of their classroom window before going boating. The boating pond, its two islands and the boats peacefully tied up were quite visible. Their entire class and Mrs Gunn had not had a very concentrated maths lesson but had spent a lot of the last part of the morning laughing at the two fools larking round on the boats in full view of the school. As a matter of fact, all the classes along the top floor on that side had been watching and marvelling at the stupidity of the truants. Mother had given the number of the phone installed for Father's 'on call' at work, for emergency use only and the school office had called her. Lennie's home had no phone, but he was not a very looked after boy at home so would probably have got a sound beating. Strangely Jon did not get the tawse. Mrs Gunn had decided that she would leave matters to his parents. Mother did not let him stay in school that afternoon, which was another mercy for the humiliation would have been complete but she took him home and sent him up to his room. The only thing she said was;

'Wait till your father gets home.'

Jon heard his father come in the door and dreaded what was going to happen because thumping was common in this household. He set his bedside cabinet as a barricade against the door and put his weight to it to stop Father from getting in, but he was a featherweight and Father pushed his way in with ease. He found his son weeping with terror, but did not hit him. This was different.

He had a belt in his hand, sat down on the bed and put it down, and then he said;

'I'm not going to belt you. I should and you deserve it, don't you?'

Jon agreed that he did. Father continued quietly and most definitely. Jon was never to play truant again. That was to be a promise - Jon agreed. That was the easy bit because it was not a habitual practice of his anyway. Then came the hard bit. Father told him that Lennie was not his friend, that he was bad for Jon and that he did not like him being friends with Lennie. He was not to go round with Lennie. He was not to speak with Lennie. In fact, if Father heard that he had any conversation with Lennie or had gone anywhere with him, then he would take the belt to him, buckle end on his bottom. Did Jon understand?
He did. Very much.

The next day Lennie was not in class. He had been moved to another one. Jon saw Lennie in the yard at break, but Lennie looked away from him with his eyes down and walked away. Jon worked out that Lennie had probably been through something similar to what he had just been having. The mental torture and shame of having been caught, the harsh and mocking teasing of some of the other kids, and the fear of Father with the belt were enough to set the seal on the end of this friendship. Life is full of such; it is probably true that Lennie was just someone to hang around with, that they reinforced each other's need for someone to talk to, but true friends are hard to find, harder to recognise and to be prized - and life is not full of those. Probably in leading an impressionable Jon into things he would not otherwise have done - or was it the other way round - they were not friends to each other in any true sense but companions in misadventure. For some time to come Jon had no boon companion.

It was of no matter because he had learned a certain self-reliance and was quite capable of going places himself now and did so when the mood or his need took him. A favourite place was Sutherlands down near the Post Office. As you left the back door of the school in Sinclair Street, past the portico, which had once been the main entrance, there was a sign on the wall 'Sutherland's Steam Bakery' at the corner of

Davidson's Lane. Their shop was where Jon liked to go. As a very rare treat Mother had been known to take Gill and himself in there, to have a cup of tea and an iced fancy cake in their tea room, and once Jon was very glad of it. Mr Bews the butcher was in Sinclair Street also and Mother had gone there on her way to town, Gill and Jon in tow. As she chatted to Mr Bews, who was a friendly man and an excellent butcher whom Mother swore by, Jon was bored. Just by the door was a big paper sack full of dog biscuits shaped liked bones. Jon's hand wandered in and he picked one of the biscuits up to have a look at it.

'You hungry wee man? Have a bite,' said Mr Bews.

Jon was indeed hungry, but he displayed a certain caution and did not take a huge bite – he just nibbled off a small corner and chewed it. It tasted of a very strong sort of Oxo and to his young mouth was far too strong a flavour.

'Yeugh! Yeugh!' he said and ran outside spitting the biscuit into the gutter. He did not feel sick but it was not a nice taste. Mr Bews laughed, and so did Mother.

'Woof, Woof,' said the butcher, but Jon did not see any humour in the situation, though the grownups thought it hilarious. Mother said that she would put him on a lead, and then they went to get on with her shopping. Into Sutherlands they went and Mother sat down at one of the little tables and ordered tea and cakes. They came on a three tiered chrome plated cake stand on lacy doilies, shiny iced and brightly coloured with waxy sweet icing outside and soft sponge on the inside. The taste of the Bonio biscuit soon receded.

This was not the reason why Jon went to Sutherland's on his own though - and it was not for their superb bread and cakes either. In Sutherland's worked a genius who could make toffee. The toffee was allowed to caramelise and was mixed into a state that would set very hard when poured. When this was set into tin foil tart cases and a stick placed in it before the toffee hardened, then you had a Sutherland's 'everlasting lolly'. There was a craze for them in the school and the shop was selling all they could make. They were a bit like traditional bonfire toffee and they did last a very long time – delicious.

Jon went into Hamish Cameron's at any excuse and at the drop of a hat not necessarily to buy anything but because he loved it in there. Take a step through the door and take a deep sniff. The smell was of coffee initially, from the great metal grinder on the counter and from the bins of coffee beans behind it. But then other smells came in from the meat slicer where the great hams or sausages would be sliced as thick as you wished it to be set, falling from the round blade onto sheets of white greased paper. Packets of crackers, of fine teas, biscuits, jars of pickles and tins of luxury soups laded the shelves. To call Hamish Cameron's a delicatessen would be foreshadowing too much, though it comes close, but to describe it as a general grocer falls far too short though the sign over the windows said 'Grocer and Wine Merchant'. The jewel in the crown was that there was no till operated by the assistant. Your money was placed into a container and attached to wires overhead along which it shot into a cubicle, wherein a cash desk and cashier. There it was deposited and the change placed in the container and returned to the assistant. Service was slow but you didn't care. What style! What class!

Just along Traill Street was the Royal Hotel and how Jon wanted to go in there but could not. It was posh, but perhaps that should be set into capital letters for looking through the window you could see a tartan carpet in red green and gold, waiters and snowy tablecloths. It would have been so nice just to walk through the revolving door to have a look but he dared not. The Royal was stayed in by bigwigs and VIPs and was very expensive. Money formed its own impenetrable barrier at the door.

Over the road from that was Kennedy's the drapers where Mother used to go to buy clothes, especially gloves and scarves. There was a nice smell of new cloth wafted out as the door opened but although Mother bought small things there, generally she did not favour buying clothes in Thurso. The Highland premium was in full force and she preferred to wait for the annual visit down south when things could be obtained much cheaper. This may have been harsh on the local shopkeepers, but with her budget she, and many others like her, could not be blamed.

Where Traill Street turned and became Olrig Street was a café - a right and proper café with a hissing coffee machine, hot milk spout and a thing that made milkshakes with a whirl of cream on the top. They also did a remarkably large ice cream sundae with splendid ice cream. This was Cardosi's Café where Jon went when he was feeling flush. Outside it was vertical wood panelling and inside it was mock wood veneer and Formica and it seemed like the essence of cool and chic. Cardosi's got a fair share of Jon's pocket money when he was living in the land beyond the north wind because they also appeared to own the fish and chip shop where Swanson Street met High Street and many a bag of chips was eaten in the street round there to supplement home rations.

Walking down the High Street you came to the Town Hall, which was a large and ornate Victorian building blackened with age, grime and rain. It also housed the geological and sample collection of a man called Robert Dick. Jon and his friends of course found Mr Dick's name hilarious for the usual schoolboy reasons but this was tempered with a certain respect for he had obviously been a man of some fame and reputation, as witnessed by his grave in the local cemetery which they had seen. It was a large obelisk, which stood out from most, and indicated someone of importance. Jon went in to look at the collection once and it was interesting for a few minutes, but being stones, fossils and objects behind glass with no buttons to press, and no great attractions for someone under 10 he had not stayed long.

There was a great excitement in the whole town when FW Woolworths opened a shop next to the Town Hall. Thurso did not have such a shop and many of the locals felt that it was some sort of sign that the town had finally 'arrived'.

'It will be Marks and Spencer's next!' they said to each other, more in hope than belief. As the only thing even resembling a department store in town it was a completely new concept to many of the locals, though there was another branch in the county town 21 miles away. The novelty of it filled the store with crowds during its first few days after opening and it was a proper 'Woolies'. The floor was narrow boards rather like a ship's deck, covered in thick hard varnish with a certain tangy polish to them the aroma of which hit your nose as you walked through the door. Counters ranged up and down, with mostly girls behind them in walkways, and in each was a till. Customers walked in and the counters were divided into rectangles of varying sizes by upright green glass partitions. In each divided area were things to buy with the price in red on a white background, clipped into a shiny chrome frame. Jon's attention was caught by the toy counter and in the various compartments were buses, cars, harmonicas, pencil sharpeners, kazoos, yo-yos, marbles, cap guns and so on. The store had a wide range of consumer goods for sale and at Woolie's prices, which did not have a Highland premium. Underwear, socks, items of clothing, glasses, plates, cutlery - you could outfit a house from what was in this store and on that day, in many of the pre-existing local shops the mark-up must have been reduced considerably and quickly. For a while at least Woolies became the throbbing commercial heart of the town, always thronging with shoppers six days a week.

On the seventh day Thurso was dead. Everything was closed and still. The churches were full, and even Mother went to church a few times. She was a confirmed member of the Church of England and always believed in her religion. There was no Church of England here since they lived firmly in Scotland, but the Scottish Episcopalian Church was, Mother assured Jon, the same. Since he was old enough to behave himself she took him there once. It was a fairly traditional looking church with a round turret for a spire outside and an arched Gothic interior. If you faced the front the view was impressive down the church. Old style pews in polished dark wood were set off nicely by a bright red carpet and there was a big shiny set of organ pipes down on the right. There was a carved wooden pulpit on the left and it was from there that the priest in his robes spoke to the congregation. At first Jon was fine – Mother had told him that he had been christened into the Church and had a right to be there. He listened to what was said, did as he was told and could sing the hymns because they were the sort that you sang in class sometimes in the mornings. A turning point came for him as people began to get out of their seats and line up in front of the priest. As Jon watched they began to eat something the priest gave them and drink from a cup. He whispered and asked mother what it was and she replied 'It's the body and blood of Jesus'.

He did not like that idea at all – not one little bit. He was feeling a bit queasy at the thought of what he might have to do, but did not wish to be left out of what was going on. When it came to Mother's turn to get up, he also got up but she hissed at him to sit down. He could not come because he was not 'confirmed.' Only people who had been confirmed could take Communion. Jon was not sure whether he should be glad or not. On the one hand he was happy and relieved that he would not to have to be a cannibal, especially if what the people were eating and drinking was not cooked, but on the other hand he was resentful. Here was something happening and he was not allowed to take part in it. His native bloody mindedness came to the surface and his uppermost thought was that if he was not allowed to take part, then he did not wish to. It is true that after her burst of enthusiasm Mother did enrol Jon and Gill for the Sunday school. It is also true that although the girl who ran it was very nice, Jon and Gill were not very interested, but by that time it did not matter. Mother had lost interest in going to the church and told them that they did not have to go back which they were happy about because going to school five days a week was already enough without an hour more on Sundays. It seemed that she had had an argument with the priest and told him that he was too High Church, and that she did not approve. There were apparently some high words on this matter, though Jon did not really understand what the matter was, and Mother did not ever go back to the Church at all except on one occasion – but that was a rather special event.

The pub was not an institution that Mother and Father used very much and not at all in Scotland. Father was never much of a pub man and although many of the men on the estate took themselves off to View Firth social club or a local bar for a drink, he tended to stay at home. There was not so much money around to spare for drink then, but Mother, who had once, when living in England, liked a night out with friends occasionally, now never went out. It is true that the same reasons of economy did apply to her, but the position of women as regards drinking in Thurso was not one of equal terms with men. A story that did the rounds among the newly arrived Power Station workers was of a woman, fresh from England in 1957 who went into the saloon bar of a local hotel because she felt like a sherry - very respectable. To her surprise she found that it was full of men and only men. As she walked to the bar, all the men in the room either finished their pints and left or simply left their drinks and walked out. The last man at a table stood up, walked up to her and said;

'You ******* hoor,' and spat in her face before leaving.

Urban myth it might have been, but it was known that some of the local men were not as up to date in their attitudes as they might have been regarding the status of women, and the story, true or not, had a powerful deterrent effect on Mother and her friends. Jon did not know what a hoor was so he asked his pals – they did not know either, but Mother did not like it obviously.

They did go out very occasionally on special days like their birthdays or the odd dance – Mother liked to dance but Father was not so keen. There was one place that they were very fond of when they could afford it. A new restaurant opened at the small harbour village of Scrabster, which was about 2-3 miles from their house. It was called the Upper Deck and Father was invited to attend the opening evening because he got a ticket given to him at work, who were paying for the food. Jacket and tie and best frock went out of the door and came home later in the evening; Joan had been babysitting Jon and Gill and they were still up when Mother and Father returned. With them they had a small paper plate of bread with all sorts of things on top. This was apparently called Smorgasbord and was a Danish sandwich though the bread tasted funny and was nearly black. Jon thought it rather silly that it did not have any bread on top and so it was not a sandwich at all. If you did not hold it level then all the filling would fall out. Mother and Father were quite merry, laughing a lot and let the children eat the smorgasbord. It was quite delicious with fish, and prawns and shrimps and little bits of meat and pickle and cheese, but still they thought it would have been easier to eat with a top slice. Smorgasbord became for a long time a feature in the house. It was served at parties and it was served for lunch on ordinary bread. Later on, as Mother spent more and more time 'on a diet' she began to do smorgasbord on Ryvita crispbread but somehow it was not the same after that.

Gill liked dancing too and for a time went to Highland dancing lessons which mother arranged for her in town. She had a little kilt to wear and was very choosy when it came to selecting a pin for it. One of the things she wanted to do was the sword dance but she had no swords - it seemed that some of the other little girls had a pair of small swords that they crossed on the floor and danced round. Father listened to this quandary very carefully and saw that his practical skills would be needed for this. At work the following day he picked up two pieces of wood that had once formed part of a cable drum and brought them home. He spent days on them working with a knife, a spoke shave and sandpaper and ended up with two virtually identical wooden swords which he then varnished. They were quite beautiful things with a lot of craftsmanship to them and Gill loved them, taking them proudly to her dance classes, and even crossing them on the living room floor and deftly floating her feet in between their 'blades' with her hands in the air.

For Jon the best place in town was the cinema to which he first went at Christmas for a school treat in 1960. He had been warned by older friends not to sit under the balcony edge so it was with some relief that he saw that his class were placed under the balcony but away from the edge. The film chosen to show the school was not the most educational that might have been picked but it was entertaining. It was the Lavender Hill Mob starring Alec Guinness. Both London and Paris were utterly foreign to Jon and probably to most of the children in the auditorium, but it seemed to engage the attention of most of them, even the older kids from upstairs. The amount of foreign matter thrown down from above was minimal on this occasion with one half tub of ice cream landing on a girl, a few sweet papers and a few people spat on, but Jon had none such. The experience was, on the whole, a good one and he decided that he would like to go to the cinema again.

It was a nice, atmospheric place with red plush seats, a little worn, and a red pattern carpet. Down the side were shell shaped white uplighters on the walls whilst at the front a glowing white clock showed the time.

By 1961 Jon's parents were convinced that the town was safe, so in response to his repeated requests to be allowed to go to the cinema with Gill they gave him more pocket money and sent them off to see Hans Christian Anderson, a Disney film starring Danny Kaye, telling the story of the great fairy tale writer. They had strict instructions to be back by 9.30 pm. It was a long programme and an interval came at 9.15 pm and Jon saw with a sinking heart that they would have to go. Father would get very angry if he were disobeyed so with a very tearful Gill in tow because she wanted to see the end, they trudged home. When Father asked her why she was crying she said that she had wanted to see the end but had to come home as the picture did not finish until after ten o'clock. Father adjusted his views on the cinema after that – he took them to see the film the following night, so that one had a happy ending. After that Jon was allowed to go to the cinema with friends – and stay until the end. For an eight year old this was generous – and liberty.

He and a friend went to see Spartacus and got themselves some prime seats as the film started, in the middle under the balcony. They thought they were in for a grand time and a good view but the tide was high and the fishing boats had just come in. Some of the trawlermen also wanted to see Spartacus and had come straight from the boats. The stench of fish and guts was truly astonishing. Jon and his pal Willy looked at each other and Willy whispered, 'Boak! Let's move.'

So they did see Spartacus - right to the end - but from side seats, which was probably not fair enough but what can eight year olds do against fish scales and guts?

Summer Holiday was better, and better yet it was released in January 1963 and Jon was 10. This was a significant birthday and Father decided that Jon should celebrate it in style but not until the snow disappeared which happened at the end of the month. He gave him a ten-shilling note to spend what he needed, and he arranged after school to meet three of his friends outside Cardosi's chip shop. There were tables and chairs in there and they all had fish and chips at a cost of four shillings the lot. Then off to the cinema in Sir George's Street, just down from the Post Office. Sixpence each and in they went. Cliff Richard was young, cool and hip and he was a bus driver and the notion of taking a red British bus to Greece seemed to be a very good idea to Jon. It went to foreign countries, not in the past but today, and the characters were people that you could relate to. Cliff, obviously because he was the hero, but the love interest did not appeal much to Jon - he was never fooled by Barbara pretending to be a boy - she would never fool anyone. But Melvyn Hayes fascinated him because he was like a young person but with an old face, while he liked the look of Una Stubbs. Jon had not thought of sex at all at this stage and did not recognise that he actually fancied the actress but to him she seemed like fun and the sort of person to be around - better than the boring lascies he knew. Above all, the idea of going down to Greece, where the sea was blue and the sun was shining and warm was going to appeal to all the boys from Thurso where much of the year round the sky was grey and the air full of water. The music was pretty cool too and Cliff was constantly topping the charts so it was much the sort of thing the lads wished to see.

As a way to celebrate your 10th birthday, it was memorable. When he got home Jon gave Father four shillings change and thought that for his first ever night out on his own treating friends, he had done pretty well – a good feed and a good flick were just the job.

More memorable even than this was an end to Jon's hopping the bottom wall of the school. You were not supposed to do it, but as a way onto Janet Street and onto the grass down to the river it was a good shortcut, but one particular evening Jon jumped on top of the wall and down onto the pavement just missing a man who was lying on the pavement, reinforcing that you should always look before you leap. The man seemed to be asleep and had been sick which was fairly disgusting and Jon wondered what on earth he had been eating because his vomit looked like coffee grounds mixed with blood. He had wet his trousers and there was a puddle of pee in which he was lying while he made a snoring noise. He stank of pee, of vomit – and of whisky. His clothes were dirty and old, his face unshaven and an empty bottle with a Haig label lay by his left hand. Jon was not exactly afraid but he did not know what to do, never having faced anything like this before; it was an intrusion of the nasty grownup world into the sheltered and protected child cocoon that he and his playmates lived in. For a moment he stood, wondering, then a man and a woman came round the corner of Lovers Lane, which led down from the station. Grown-ups! They would take care of it so Jon took to his heels and fled. For whatever reason it put him off jumping the wall and he preferred to leave school after that via the Paterson's lane exit which was fine as it led directly into town. Town was his and all that was in it, and he swam in its environs as a fish swims in the sea, whilst in turn he was the town's, now and always, for whilst you may take the boy out of Thurso, you can never take Thurso out of the boy, no matter how grey his head.

Out and About

Father had bought a car. It was an Austin 10. The main reason he had bought it was to go to work, but also because the train tickets were so expensive to go back to Cumberland for holidays and the petrol was cheaper. The logical answer was a car, so the old Austin was just the ticket. He had it for a few months before the summer holiday of 1959 but Mother did not appreciate it much. There was a lot of rust in the car and when it rained and they went through puddles, water splashed up through a hole and wet her feet. The answer was to put a sheet of cardboard down over the hole, but clearly this car was not going to last very long.

Now that Father had a car it became possible to explore the area much more widely; he and Mother were not great walkers so although they would go for a walk round town, they did not have any wish to explore the wider area on foot or by bike. Having a car liberated them and Jon and Gill also. It is a pity that they were not adventurous enough ever to take the ferry over to Orkney, but given their income it is possible that Father simply could not afford it – and Mother did not work at all except at home - that was her job. In the car though, Hyperborea was theirs to explore, whether a short run out to Janetstown, then to Halkirk and Loch Calder's grey ripples, out to back of Watten in the rain, or longer excursions, for the whole area was now open to them.

A favourite place to explore was the county town of Wick largely because it had shops that were different, apart from the great grey colonnade of Woolworths with the clock on the top. Like Thurso, Wick was a place that bustled with many shops of a wide variety and the prosperity and business of the place was apparent as soon as you crossed the bridge. It was a graceful town and although the shopping centre was rather smaller than Thurso it was attractive. Most people in those days did not have fridges at home but a larder or a 'cold cupboard' with a wire gauze door to keep insects out. If people wanted fresh produce then they tended not to keep it in the house but went out to shop every day. This meant that town centres were busy places that bustled as women with shopping bags, kids in tow, went about their daily business in much the same way as they had for decades and would do

79

until the late 60s when the spread of supermarkets and the wholesale purchase of fridges by most of the population brought stillness to the small town centres.

Mother was not fond of Wick at first because shortly after she arrived in Caithness she needed an extraction and it was a wisdom tooth. Father drove Mother over to Wick under a darkling sky late one afternoon and into a street down near the harbour and the children waited in the car as Father said they would not be long. They were in fact ages and Mother had had a hard time of it. The anaesthetic had worked well enough but the dentist could not draw the tooth. He pulled and pulled and it took nearly an hour before he could wiggle it out. Mother said that the root was like a corkscrew screwed into her jaw which was why he had trouble and that this was hereditary – Jon's teeth might be like it too. He hoped not because Mother was looking as if she had gone several rounds in the ring with boxing gloves. She was very cross and kept on talking about the experience for weeks calling the dentist;

'A bloody hoss doctor,' and she did not go there again, finding a dentist in Thurso.

Jon liked Wick because he had won his speaking certificate there. He also liked the harbour – it was far bigger than Thurso's and it was packed with North Sea drifters, little wooden boats fit to voyage far out and then use their rear sail to provide what way they needed whilst they fished. The harbour bustled with lorries, there were fish baskets everywhere, some with silvery herring in ice just laying there, and everywhere coils of rope, netting and large round fishing floats. Reeking lorries, heavy-laden, drove off in diesel fumes to take the fish off way down the A9 to points south whilst weather beaten men in sweaters did important things in and around the boats. Down River Street and Martha Terrace you could walk, across the bridge and onto the shore and be stepping over boat ropes all the way, double and triple moored out into the harbour.

After a stroll round Wick and buying a few things it was back to the car and out to the south along the A9 (now A99) coast road. Inland were moors sweeping into the distance, heather and bog but the coast had a strip of green grass clinging to the edge and sloping down to the sea. As the car thrummed down the tarmac towards Lybster numerous white croft buildings were dotted round the landscape between the moor and the edge of the world where the grey North Sea stretched away into infinity. From the chimney of each a plume of smoke rose and a strange acrid smell pervaded the air. The source of these was to be found beside each croft where a neat black pile of soft peat bricks stood drying in the open air. Mother called them peat haggs and Jon got terribly confused thinking that somewhere beside or inside each was hiding an old crone, for he knew the word hag from fairy tales. Once he realised that there were two Gs the fear and the image vanished but while they lasted the old witches were a formidable picture.

If you were lucky, then you might see a great ship heading on its way, slowly churning to foreign harbours and far away lands, but you had to be especially lucky to see what Jon did on this day. A couple of miles off shore or so it seemed the low and dangerous shape of a Royal Navy ship sped her way southwards, a bone in her teeth and the wind in her tail.

'A destroyer!' breathed Jon having read about such things – and he liked the name anyway.
Father, who should have been watching the road said;
'No – it's a frigate.'
There was no more explanation than that but Father knew everything so he must be right. Not wishing to show ignorance Jon said nothing but decided he would look up frigate when he got home in his dictionary. Sure enough it was there;

'Frigate - a small fast warship for escort and anti-submarine duties.'

So there! He did not see what the difference was between a destroyer and a frigate but obviously there was one and he had seen a frigate. One day he would see a destroyer.

As a place to see Lybster was not much for Jon and Gill to get excited about The town or rather village was basically one street and quite attractive, but the romance was to be found at the harbour. That was the place to go. There are places, which are simply evocative and the harbour at Lybster one was of these. Driving down the sloping road

81

between green grass banks studded with cow parsley you came to a harbour where boats could come from the sea, up a channel and turn into a completely closed in harbour, safe from all harm. Between the boats and the open sea stretched a broad and flat expanse of concrete which functioned as a fish quay in days of yore while a couple of warehouse buildings, deserted now, stood over the road. From the concrete quay a grey stone mole stretched seawards protecting the channel from filling up with longshore drift and at the extreme end of which a larger ship could berth on the seaward side. It was buttressed with concrete and had a raised walkway and at the seaward end was a small lighthouse at the edge of the channel, painted white with a lamp revolving, sending small shafts of illumination out into the grey of the sea, signalling to lost seals the way home. To Jon's pleasure there was a small ship tied up on the other side of the mole right at the end. To his eye she looked like a great ocean going craft but in fact she probably was a small cargo vessel plying the North Sea coast up and down, calling at small ports with goods – as many used to in such harbours. She was a neat painted miniature ship in all details and looked as if she could take any thing the ocean threw at her.

It was cold and the dark was coming so Father said that they had to go and the car wended its way back up to the main road, turned left and headed for Latheron, the A895 (now A9) across the Causeymire, and home.

Jon liked the Causeymire when he crossed it in either train or car. It was part of the Flow Country – the great flat wilderness of heather and lakes carved out by glaciers 10,000 years ago and scoured by outwash waters. Now it was covered in a thick blanket of heather and the wind blew across its treeless expanse free and unfettered. There was not a building or a tree in sight, yet in the car heading home with the lowering darkness from the east, a strong wind scudding from the north and pulses of rain and mist skating over the whole scene, Jon caught his breath and looked at a cold bleak wilderness of such beauty that it could break your heart with the fierceness of it. It was so elemental, so natural, and so clean that it quite took the words from you and all power of expression was lost in the face of its presence, like observing the raw power of God made plain upon the landscape. It was good that it was so, for a building on the Causeymire would have been a blasphemy fit for the Furies to be set upon to avenge. He loved this place, hard, cold and unforgiving and his love for it was also hard because it cleaned your soul and told you what was important. The very raw savagery of it set off how precarious was life and all its comforts and worries, how transitory and passing.

It was strange how the landscape changed as soon as the Causeymire was crossed. The wild hyperborean wilderness gave way all of a sudden as if passing out of a shadowland between one world and the next, to rolling green pastureland of a much gentler hue. Still washed by rain but softer and tamer, the road rose between fields to a junction where right was Wick and left was Thurso - seven miles to civilisation, shops, estates and comforts. In another way the whole area on the north east tip of Hyperborea was protected from the demons of the outside world by a wide strip of moor threaded by few roads, and daunting to outsiders. Jon liked how cut off it was from the rest of the world, its remoteness and its honesty.

Along the road to Thurso, almost dark by now with mist and rain driving onto the windscreen and a fog upon the inside of the car windows because it was cold outside and warm within. Suddenly Thurso cemetery is on the left and the streetlights begin, and the banshees of the moor and the wind and the rain are left behind as the car runs down to the bridge under sodium orange streetlights, across the bridge and quickly to home. Get the fire going and a nice cup of tea to end a great and adventurous day. Can there be a feeling like it anywhere else or as good as this in the entire wide world?

It is the end for the Austin A40 though, as Mother's feet were wet and the piece of cardboard on the floor was sodden and soggy. A better car they had to have. Father went out and came back with a 1948 Hillman Minx Estate in darkest Prussian blue; Jon knew it was Prussian blue because that was what Mrs Gunn called it at school when he painted a policeman one afternoon and wanted to get the colour right. Father did not have a good track record with buying cars, even though he was a qualified mechanical engineer. It was a lovely car, shiny and plenty of room in side, with a strange profile that the children liked because it was so different, but it was doubtful if anyone but Father could have kept it going. As it was he spent more and more time outside fiddling under the bonnet and eventually got fed up with it refusing to start, stopping running at odd moments and being a mechanical pig so he traded it in within a very short time for a greenish Morris Traveller van. The children loved it for its roominess, its reliability and the wooden framework of it which was distinctive, and it did not break down even if Father kept adjusting its tappets, whatever they were.

On a Sunday afternoon a long walk might just be in order up over Pennyland and down the road towards Scrabster. In total this cannot be more than about three miles there and three miles back but it feels longer. There is a pavement all the way as the A882 (now A9) branches away down towards the harbour as the A836 continues out along the north coast heading for Durness. To be wary of, at the junction was a collection of low caravans huddling together in a dip where Father says the 'Tinks' live. Why you should be wary Jon was not sure because he had met a few Tinks and they seemed all right to him. He once asked Father what Tinks were and Father told him that they travelled round all over the place and did not live in houses. This seemed fair enough to Jon who quite liked the notion of living in a caravan instead of a house. Recently he had bought for himself 'The Wind in the Willows' in which Toad, Ratty and Mole go off with a horse and a gypsy caravan and the romance of it appealed to him. But best of all was when he asked Father where the Tinks came from and Father said that many people thought that they were descended from sailors of the Spanish Armada. Jon knew about that – he had heard the story from Mrs Gunn, how sailors from the great Armada had been washed ashore and how many had been murdered while some lucky ones had made new lives for themselves among the people they found themselves with. That sort of did it for Jon – if Tinks were descended from the Armada then his imagination clothed them with Spanish faces, Morion helmets, aquiline noses and haughty demeanours – he had seen those films too and he thought them quite cool.

Scrabster lay low and the A882 (now A9) swept down to it, descending in an arc round and down a slope with a few houses dotted on the brow but nothing of any consequence at all between the town and the harbour. One you had passed the Thurso sign at Pennyland there was not a single dwelling all the way down to Scrabster. The harbour village was small and dominated by the gleaming metal drums of the Shell oil depot which was built on an infill which had once been sea but was now hard grey stone chippings dumped where the water had been and embanked down into a damp depression before rising up again to a sort of grey stone band that held the sea back; it looked as if someone had had the idea that at some point in the indefinite future this depression might be filled in to make more land. Most of the buildings huddled along the base of the steep slope up to the top of the cliff where perched a few bungalows. Prominent among them was a dingy old ships chandler stores, which served the small fishing fleet in the harbour – and the spanking new and modern Upper Deck restaurant where Mother and Father liked to go. The small harbour was packed with drifters and all the paraphernalia of a small fishing port – and all the smells too.

The real interest came as you progressed along towards the lifeboat, which was just beyond the last harbour wall, at the start of the track leading up to the lighthouse. It was a white painted corrugated iron structure with a slipway leading down to the water and the lifeboat's nose poking down the slope ready to go. Jon never saw it go down but he wanted to. It was hardly likely that he ever would because such a dramatic act normally took place in heavy weather when spectators were few and far between, being safely tucked up indoors. All round the bay you could not avoid knowing when the lifeboat was about to go though; most people did not have phones, even lifeboat men and the first thing that people knew that the boat was to launch was a massive 'crack' that was heard all over town. The first time Jon heard it he immediately turned his eyes to the air above the sea, following the sound and saw a puff of smoke where an explosion had just taken place. Father told him that it was a maroon or big rocket that was sent up to get the lifeboat-men to report immediately. The only maroon that Jon knew was the colour so he thought that the big rocket was that colour ever after - and maybe it was.

Over the sea wall, people fished with rods and handlines. You could see down through water as clear as glass right to the bottom, and looking very carefully, you could see flat fish nosing along the white sand. One day Father decided that it would be a good idea to supplement the family diet with some fish so he and Jon went to the chandlers and Father bought a wooden hand-reel with orange line, two silvery round weights with little studs on them, and several hooks. Father had some

85

bread which he moulded into doughy pellets and lowered the line carefully into the water. Sure enough, before too long he had four small flatfish, which he put into a bag. Jon wanted a go, but he looked down into the water and saw a fearsome sight. There was a monster down above the flatfish. Father said that it was a conger eel and it had a fierce looking face, big teeth and was about as long as half a telegraph pole – the boy not know that eels could grow that long. Nevertheless, he wanted a go with the hand-reel and hoped that the eel would not take the bait because he did not wish to be dragged into the water and be bitten. Father would not let him have a go but said that he would have to wait until he caught another fish. This did not seem very fair as the adult had already caught several fish, but children have no choice in such matters so Jon had to accept it willy-nilly. Father thought the bigger flatfish were further out so he braced himself and whirled the line flinging the weights out as far as he could. Then he accidentally let go of the reel and the whole thing sailed into the water.

Jon was literally hopping up and down with anger and disappointment, indeed pure juvenile rage, because he had not had his go. The reel was floating in the water about 10 feet below where he stood and he reasoned that if they went home in the car and came back with the rake from the garden then they could hook it out fairly easily, but Father laughed and said it was not worth it - he would buy another. He never did; Father and son went home and Mother fried the flatfish for dinner after rolling them in flour. They were quite delicious and very fresh, but they were the last fish caught in that family.

Past the lifeboat station the road ended and a path could be followed towards the end of Holborn Head. Lighthouses were a source of romance to young boys but perhaps not to the people who worked them. As night drew on over Thurso Bay Jon liked to see the beam from Holborn lancing out into the dusk, being answered by a flash in the distance from the light at Dunnet Head far away, the most northerly point of the British mainland. Beams of light in a gathering sea of darkness they offered safety and waymarks for sailors and passengers on vessels going through the Pentland Firth. Father had said that this was one of the most dangerous stretches of water in the entire world, with massive storms and waves of up to 20 feet where the Atlantic ocean met the North Sea and the tide raced faster than anywhere else.

The waves were so powerful he said, that in storms stones had been thrown up that broke the windows of the lighthouse 380 foot above sea level.

On a fine bright yellow sunlit afternoon, on the grassy bank above the lighthouse it was a grand thing to sit on the grass and chew a straw and watch the St Ola come in. This was the ferry, which ran from Scrabster to Stromness in the Orkneys; by ferry standards she was not perhaps too large, having space for 30 cars and 300 passengers, but to Jon she looked like the Queen Elizabeth. It seemed impossible that a ship so large would ever get into the harbour but she did, gliding effortlessly between the edges of the port to tie up at the long pier. He would have loved to go on her over to Orkney to see what those distant isles were like that he could see from his house. He expected wild windswept heather moorland such as surrounded Hyperborea and would have been very surprised to see the soft green cattle country of Orkney had he made it over there. Even despite the money situation, had they been able to afford to go, it was doubtful if they would have got Mother on the boat. She had watched the St Ola forging through some heavy weather once, her bows dipping in and out of the waves as she dipped and rose in the violence of them, and she said just looking at it made her feel sick.

Nothing more to see as the people came off, so might as well continue the walk out to the head of the promontory. It's a long way up from the sea here and the path threads narrowly past deep blowholes, from which can be heard a subterranean roaring as of some great dragon in the depths. In bad weather when the great waves pound against the coast plumes of white water and foam shoot up out of these dark abysses that made Jon shudder to look at them. Not far down inside one of these holes is a ledge and on it was a dead sheep decaying in awful stench and not a place to linger. There is a thin soil and here on the edge of land the grass is coarse, the heather whipped over by constant wind and the rocks are black, hard and forbidding. At the end of the world the way narrows to the smallest nose on which you can stand with sea on three sides. To your left is a black and layered cliff of rocks as old as the world, stygian black and falling into a foaming screaming chaos of spume and fury. In front is the wide expanse of the sea, the isles of the North in clear view, the Old Man of Hoy hunkering close to the side of the nearest; and to the right the wide expanse of the bay, broad waves tumbling towards Thurso beach and running up river at high tide. There is a dreadful lure to the lip and the walker is tempted down to look over, but it is best not to with any sort of wind, and there is always wind. It is not a place to hang round but somewhere for a small boy to fear, to be glad of turning away from, and to retreat down the path with a shudder at the ill feel of it. So back along the harbour, quiet now and sleepy, up the road with its low and peculiar walls bounding the fields, made of slabs of flat Caithness stone stood on end like tombstones covered in patches of orange lichen, back up to Pennyland and the civilised softness of the Atomic estates with their clean rain-washed houses, their green spaces and their regular sharp and modern lines.

On another day the expedition might be in the car and off into the hinterland. Running to the east from Thurso the car slowed down as it reached Castletown where live very hardy folk. It was summer it is true, but it was cold and it had just hailed quite hard as if it were winter, which it was not for August is undoubtedly summer. Perhaps living in Hyperborea still held its surprises and Jon by now was fairly used to the cold, but he was in a warm car in long trousers, anorak and good shoes. The inhabitants of Castletown were playing football and running round in short sleeved shirts and shorts. Ah well, no matter – he did not have to do it so he was not bothered, though it did impress him. One man's nippy cold is another's mild summer day. Down through the long street they trundled, turning left at the end and down into a flatter area, across the stream by a large old mill house, deserted that Jon always thought looked like a splendid place for ghosts, then into the desert.

Of course it was not really a desert but to the children it looked that way because the road went more or less straight behind the great white-pale-gold sand dunes that formed the back of Dunnet beach. For a great distance inland the wind had, over thousands of years, blown the sand and a large area was covered with it and in turn taken over by huge clumps of long deep rooted marram grass that held it in place. You did not have to go to the other end by Dunnet village because there were a couple of places that the car could pull off the road into wired enclosures, you could climb the stile over and into the dunes area and wend your way through numerous dragon's teeth which was the name Father gave to the hundreds regular concrete shapes that dotted the dunes and all the way down onto the sand. Apparently they were supposed to stop tanks during the war, but Jon could not quite see that they would work. Gill and Jon preferred that because you threaded your way up a path onto the top of the dunes and then found yourself looking down onto the beach which was at the bottom of soft sandy slopes that you could hurl yourself off. It did not matter that you might be 10 feet above them, you fell into soft dry sand, picked yourself up and ran off along the beach. And what a beach!

Jon stayed away from the western end of the beach. One of his friends had told him that there was quicksand at that end which would suck you down and drown you before you could blink. He did not know what quicksand was and did not wish to so stayed away from that end. No matter – it was a big beach and so much to do! This was no bathing beach though a few brave souls might try It – If you dipped your toe in the clear water the shock of it was enough to make you shiver. That was a great pity because the sand of the beach was golden, lovely and clean, the sea a beautiful shade of blue or green depending on its mood, and had it been in warmer climes it would have been a haunt of millionaires. No – this was a beachcombing beach for people like the children, those who loved cold beauty, unrequited desire, and scanning for flotsam and jetsam – oh and dog walking. Jon and Gill both loved to run along the mark left by the last tide looking for objects washed up – everything washed up at Dunnet. Fired by tales of shipwreck and smuggling Jon thought it a pity there was never the dead body of a pirate to see, but mercifully he was spared that and had to be content with other things. There was once a smashed up boat in pieces, but most of what he saw was fishing nets, floats, old plastic bottles, the odd shoe, and once a round hairy thing bigger than a human head. What on earth was it? Gill would not go near it but stuck her thumb in her mouth and stared at it. Father laughed and said it was a coconut but Jon did not think it looked much like one – he had eaten them and this was much bigger. Father explained that coconuts grew in thick coats called husks which were filled with hairy fibre and that they could float. This one had probably fallen into the sea off some island in the Caribbean and ended up here. He explained that there was a current in the sea, which came all the way, 3,000 miles across the Atlantic, that could have done this. Jon was very fond of currants and raisins and found this a bit of a distraction, but understood that Father was speaking of a different sort of current.

On an exhilarating day, a windy day, the tide might be racing in at Dunnet and the wind might be coming off the land and if it was blowing strong enough it would curl the tops of the waves back on themselves creating a sort of spray mist in the air, wetting your face and refracting sunlight so that you could hardly see the other side of the beach for a glow in the moisture. Even when flat calm it was dotted with small flat stones that you could skim. Dogfish purses, razor shells and all sorts of other shells too, though Jon never found a cowrie there. About halfway along was a stream of fresh water running out of the dunes and spreading out as it went down the beach into isles and islands, channels and runnels, which the children liked to paddle in. In the summer, as a special treat there might be an ice cream if the van was parked in the main car park, but this must not be relied on. Even in winter Dunnet beach was a treat when ice and snow caked on the sand and you could tread through it with a most satisfying crunch at every step.

The car would drive up towards Dunnet village then turn off left up a narrow road that led to Brough behind St John's Loch. This was still farmland, green and windswept, studded with a few low lying crofts and a lady who smiled and waved back as the children waved at her from the back windows of the car. It soon petered out though as the road reached the coast again at a cliff and Father stopped on the side. Quietly he got out and motioned the children over to the edge of the road overlooking the sea. There was a track going down to a small jetty and a little cove studded with boulders into which the sea washed gently. There was a building down there and a couple of boats but noone was in sight and all was completely quiet.

'Seals,' whispered Father.
'Ooooh where?' said Gill and he pointed.

It took them a while but looking carefully they saw the seals lying flat and slug-like not far from the water and then a big one hauled itself out of the water onto the slip at the end of the jetty. Gill's eyes were like saucers and they stayed a few minutes but did not go any closer. Back to the car and up to Dunnet Head they went. The land turned brown and heathery as a narrow road with passing places wound its way between lochs and tarns, up and down depressions and rises and past a great enclosed area that Jon always wanted to go into. It was apparently the garden for the lighthouse keepers and had a wooden door on it so you could not see inside. Apparently the four tall walls would keep the wind out and allow vegetables to grow in there. Going up the slope you also had to go past quite a few military buildings, which did not look that old. They had been used during the war for radar or something but you did not go near them because notices said that it was WD property and you would be persecuted if you went near them. The notices actually said prosecuted but Jon preferred persecuted because it sounded better.

Up at the lighthouse it was windy and cold and not a place to hang about. The cliff was edged with Caithness slabs and Father held Jon so he could look over and see the waves hitting the rocks at the bottom. Then he pretended to shove him over and Jon jumped backwards going 'Oeeer!' which made Father laugh loud. Gill wanted him to do it to her too but Mother got annoyed and told him not to and stalked back towards the car with her bad face on. Father followed and drove a bit shamefacedly back down the hill.

It is possible to drive down through the village at Scarfskerry and come to a place where the road passes by a low cliff where seals may be seen. The landscape here was in great sweeps of green pastureland, not far above the sea, dotted with crofts and larger farms and the narrow lanes away from the main road were long and straight, the horizon far off. These roads tempted drivers to put their speed up and go fast because in the clear visibility of the Hyperborean air you could see a very long way. The skies were big, the clouds were high and the skyline was miles away, rising as it went inland to quite a height up towards Slickly. Father had heard from a friend that there was a track down to a beach by the Castle of Mey where the seals lay out on the sand. The car bumped down a stony track, which got rougher and eventually came to a junction where the castle could be seen on the right. Mother said; 'Look – a sentry box,' and sure enough there was a little box by the road leading to the beach, which turned out to be directly seaward of the Queen Mother's castle. 'I don't think we are meant to be down here,' said Mother. Father agreed - there was noone else in sight but it had a feel of private territory though there had been no notices. 'I don't need to see any more seals anyway,' declared Father and they drove off back home for dinner.

A much more determined expedition was to Duncansby Stacks and this involved the long drive of 17 miles to John o' Groats to park at the Highland confection that was the John o' Groats Hotel. Jon always thought it looked incredibly expensive to stay there. He would have liked to only he was never likely to be able to afford it. The road to Duncansby Head later was single track with passing places, rising up gently on an inclined plane sort of landscape, featureless, green and windswept for much of the year. To the left was the long grey sweep of the coast and the grim iron waters of the Pentland Firth. Ahead the road stretched like a tape measure dropped on the land gently up, then gently down into a dip, and up again towards the lighthouse at the head. In the dip was a small parking place where a few cars could rest while their owners walked over to a drop down onto a pebble and sand beach leaving the sheep to gaze at the cars with blank expressions. It was here that you could find Groatie Buckies – the small cowrie shells that were a peculiarity of this part of the coast. They were tiny, and most no bigger than the fingernail on the smallest hand, but Mother prized them and took all she was given.

Across the choppy crests of the waves could be seen the little island of Stroma, so near, yet so far, and farther out was the unattainable tip of Brough Ness on the bottom of South Ronaldsay. It beckoned, but Jon could not go, though he would have liked to. Something there was even more compelling far out to sea and that was a double lighthouse poking out of the white topped waves distant and far beyond Jon's hopes. Few people ever have the privilege of visiting the Pentland Skerries but Jon flew there on seagull wings many times in his dreams or maybe even those of puffins, for there were many here. A cold and chilling wind makes this beach a place to move on from in a warm car so on up the road to a small parking space in view of the lighthouse at Duncansby Head on the furthest north east point of the mainland UK.

The lighthouse itself sits like a low and frosted cake, covered with Imperial icing, squat and square, painted thick white and with a very low tower for its lamp. It does not need to be high for it sits over 200 feet above the sea and out on its promontory its beams describe a circle, most of which glances out over the water. The lantern actually squats as well, quite low on its tower and hunkering behind a buff painted rampart. It may not be the most spectacular of lighthouses but the location is all of that and it did its job well. Jon was fond of lighthouses, for where they were, the romance of the job as it appeared to him, and for their light in the dark. Something else he liked at home as when it was foggy. If you listened you could hear the foghorn in the distance at Holborn Head and if you listened very carefully indeed and had the ears of a child, you could hear in the distance the foghorn of Dunnet Head answering its mate like a mournful whale looking for its wife.

A short walk up a rise and looking down and you could see Duncansby Stacks. Father, Mother, Jon and Gill walked part of the way down to the track so you could see the two stacks poking up out of the water like twin teeth and Jon asked how they had got there. It was Father who explained that they had once been part of the mainland but the sea had eaten away the land behind them, cutting them off into islands – just like the Old Man of Hoy. The boy understood that because it had been explained to him before but it was news to him that Hoy was not unique. Now he knew that there were stacks in other places.

Out to sea there was something big in the water but they could not see what it was though Mother thought it might be a whale. She said that they often got whales round this part of the coast, but with no binoculars they could not be sure. It could be a dolphin or even a killer whale. In the meantime she was bloody cold and wanted a cup of tea. So back to the car and out with the big thermos flask, tartan tin outside, two cream-yellow plastic cups and two extra in a bag, spun glass interior, and hot tea - with biscuits for them as wants them. Jon and Gill always wanted biscuits especially if there was a Tunnock's Caramel Wafer or two around. There usually was.

On another occasion in summer the family piled into the car and went south as far as Dornoch, which they had heard was a nice place. So it was, but to Jon and Gill the neatness of the town and the attractiveness of the buildings were not really their thing. What they had come for was to see the beach – and see it they did because the tide was out. The sea was blue, the sand was pure gold and there were boulders to climb. It was still quite chilly even though it was summer, but there was one boulder in particular that stood out because it was the size of a bus and somebody had affixed a diving board to it – which to Jon seemed odd because there was no water below it - when they drew closer he saw that it was about six foot above the sand so when the tide was in you would be able to jump off into a few feet of water – but not head first, or the results would be unfortunate. Gill was wearing a red cardigan, buttoned up, with grey slacks and a broad collared blouse and her hair up in 'Tweets'. Jon was in short trousers and long grey socks to below the knee held up with elastic and a white shirt under a grey V neck pullover. He posed in a climbing position on the boulder while Gill put her foot cautiously on the bottom of it and Father took their picture frozen for all time in that position. Gill called her bunches 'Tweets' because one of her friends had them and her brother used to pull them saying 'Tweet'. Brothers did that, but she became known as 'Tweets' and the name stuck.

Whatever you were doing on a Saturday in the summer though, you had to be sure of one thing. You had to be back for tea, leave time to walk down to Traill Street and find a good place to stand. It was certain that you must never ever stand under the trees on Sir John's Square, so getting a good place to stand was important. If you were before time then you would see the Thurso pipe band assemble outside Shearers the butchers on the road there and they looked absolutely magnificent in the full uniform – the Glengarry, the short jacket, the kilt, sporran stockings pumps and skein dubh. And of course the pipes; Jon could see the man from the garage at Halkirk hefting them up, and the butcher, and the man from the grocery, but they looked so different - heroes from a bygone age as they prepared for the off. Lined up, serried ranks, pipe major to the fore and off we go – 'Scotland the Brave' in measured pace down the full length of Traill Street and the cheers of the crowd roaring out. And the crowd was legion, packing the pavement; back they came to Cock of the North, the Rowan Tree, and great favourites. Gill was dancing up and down with delight for she loved the pipes dearly. There was a coach-load of Americans had pulled up in Princes Street which ran parallel to the march route and a buzz went round that that had driven up from Scrabster and a great liner that was anchored far out in the bay. They heard the pipes and flooded down in a cloud of cameras and check trousers, 'Gee! Wow!' and took up the only free space on the line of the band's march - under the trees in the square. It did not occur to them to wonder why there was noone else there in such a prime position, and noone told them, for reasons that cannot be guessed at. Bagpipes are wonderful, but they are very loud. The sombre drum beat and onward march of them in massed and warlike array is very impressive and inexorable. On the band marched, Scotland's pride, back up Traill Street – more cheers and the occasional 'Hooooooch' from men whose wives telt them off for being 'vulgar' and then the full wave of sound from 'Black Bear' hit the birds high up in the branches of the trees. A wonderful avian laxative are bagpipes and as the first rank of pipers reached the first tree the birds let their full bomb-load go in a perfect white rain of guano on whatever was underneath. Never was so much shit dropped on so many Americans in the history of Thurso – an event unparalleled in the annals of the town. The squealing and screaming as the Americans, the 'Oh my Gods', the middle aged running and hands waved in the air made Jon, Gill and hundreds of others dissolve in a mass hysteria of laughing - certainly until their sides hurt. It was a night to remember – but perhaps not for all the right reasons.

Bagpipes were very handy for another reason. It was the custom for conscientious mothers to watch out for children who had disease so when Jan from next door but one caught chicken pox Mother made sure that Jon played with him – and sure enough he caught it as well. In this way over his childhood years he had chicken pox, measles and mumps and got them out of the way while small. One of his unplanned ones was croup, which was comparatively mild, but he also had whooping cough. This one was nasty and he coughed a lot. In his room mother put a burner with a Vick's menthol dispenser in it and a small candle which filled the room with a visible vapour like an indoor fog. Inhaling this eased his breathing a lot and he was over it in about three weeks or so. Being off school compensated quite a lot for the germs. With Gill it was rather different for she also coughed a lot and had the night light in her room but could not get to sleep. Dr Giddis was rather worried about this, for with sick children he visited every day, being the best of his profession, but he did not have to worry for too long. Father had given Mother a little Dansette radio and record player – when a lid was lifted the smallest and neatest imaginable turntable was revealed and it played 45s. Mother did not have many but one of them was a 45 with Scotland the Brave on one side, and the Rowan tree on the other. One afternoon when Gill was sick she played the rowan tree and Gill fell asleep. Intrigued by this, when Gill went to bed that night Mother played the Rowan Tree to her again and to her surprise her daughter's eyes drooped. Her head went back and she went out like a light.

Next day Mother told Dr Giddis of her discovery and he laughed like a drain, thinking that she was joking – he hated the pipes, which she found surprising in a Scotsman, but he said they were loud and cacophonous. He also expressed a certain amount of disbelief as he examined Gill where she was lying on the couch near where Mother had been ironing.

'Alright' said Mother; 'Just watch this.'

Once again the Rowan Tree sounded out from the Dansette and a six year-old head began to droop and before it was finished Gill was fast asleep.

'Well I'm damned!' said Giddis. 'Bagpipes as a sedative! That's a new one – maybe I'd better write an article on that for the BMJ.'

Jon doubted that he ever did though – he was far too busy a man for such things and the area of his practice was wide. Outside Thurso the countryside stretched away, and doctors were few and far between.

Go West

Out of town the A836 had been upgraded for 10 miles and it was just as well for this was the road to the power station. Between about 7.30 am and 9.00 am it was as busy a stretch of traffic as might have been found anywhere in the UK with dozens of cars whizzing their owners and passengers to work at Dounreay. Just after 5 in the evening it was the same story if not slightly more intense for blue collar and white collar finished work at the same time if they were not on shift work. It was a proper fast A road and probably not a good place for cyclists and pedestrians at those time; at all other times, and particularly at the weekends it was quiet and sleepy. As you drove out of Thurso you might briefly think that the wild area was beginning because the land rose and got rougher, but once past this the road ran though farmland with neat ploughed fields alternating with sheep and cattle areas all the way out to Forss House where Father said there was a big old mill. This sat in a small valley, which was singular in that it had trees and Hyperborea is not renowned as a woody area though they will flourish where there is shelter for them or where they are cared for. Round the Queen Mother's Castle of Mey there was a sizeable wood and similarly up the River Thurso below the station, there were many trees but the general impression right across the area was of open windy stretches.

Once past Forss a car could race along a straight stretch with a kink to another straight stretch which Father called 'The Mad Mile' because so many people turned out of work and put their foot down in a hurry to get home and though he said he never did, Mother did not believe him.

In the hamlet of Buldoo was the entrance to an old air station of the RAF dating from World War Two. The driveway led right across the old runway to the great reactor Dome of Dounreay nuclear power station, which was where Father worked and what had brought the family north. The containment vessel for the fast reactor was an astonishing sight because it was a great sphere painted stark white sitting in the landscape, and framed against the sea almost on the very edge of the coast in a most dramatic setting. To Jon's eyes it was a potent symbol of the modern age, and it was acknowledged widely across the world to be an amazing piece of engineering. It had been built between 1955 and 1958 so it had been finished while Jon was in

Thurso but he had never seen it before it was whole. Father had though – he had been working at Dounreay from 1957 when he had moved up from Calder Hall, Britain's first atomic power station.

At that time many of the men who were working on building the station were living in barracks which were the old wartime huts of the RAF station, refurbished, heated and not very comfortable. Luckily he had not had to live there very long, and did not find it much of a hardship since up until 1953 he had been in the army and lived in a number of barracks, so it was a life he was used to. What he did not like was the high number of thefts going on there, and often said that if you did not nail something down then it would go missing. One thing he missed particularly was his old army beret, which he wore constantly in the cold winds on sit - until the day he left it on a console in the new control room, which was building, and when he came back a few minutes later, it was gone. He missed that keenly for he had worn it through his national service.

The actual building of the sphere had been an epic of construction by workers mostly from the south of Scotland, who had worked in all weathers to built the sphere which had to be lower pressure than the atmosphere inside and airlocked so that any radiation leaks would not escape - any air would be coming in rather than going out. This meant that it could not be built in bolted or riveted sections, for joints leak – it had to be constructed in such a manner that the joints were all welded and the metal formed one piece. Accordingly each specially shaped steel piece, rolled specifically for its place in a mill on site, was put into position and held by special clamps while it was expertly welded to a degree of very high precision. Before the top was put on a large stainless steel reactor vessel was landed by ship at Scrabster and brought slowly along the upgraded A road to be lifted by a huge crane over the top of the sphere, 135 feet in diameter and lowered into place. Father, though he had no part in the building of the sphere, was proud of it as most of the workers seemed to be, but he, like they, always referred to it as 'The Golf Ball'. He worked in the control room where as an electrical instruments engineer he specialised in control and instrumentation; Jon occasionally saw photos of the control room in magazines and newspapers but Father was never in them because he hated being photographed and would always avoid it wherever possible.

On 14 November 1959 Father was in the control room at Dounreay when the Dounreay fast reactor achieved criticality and it was quite late in the evening. Also working in the station that night was Bill, Aunty Joan's husband; outside there was heavy rain and wind and the occasional almighty clap of thunder.

Back in Thurso Mother was about to go to bed at about 11 o' clock when there was a frantic knocking at the door. She opened it to find a weeping Joan absolutely petrified with fear. She had never been quite sure of the difference between an atomic bomb and an atomic power station and the last great explosion in the sky and the flash had convinced her that the reactor had blown up, for she knew that something big was to happen that night. To make matters worse she had been reading in a magazine about the prophecies of the Brahan seer.

'Sheep shall eat men, men will eat sheep, the black rain will eat all things; in the end old men shall return from new lands.'

Joan knew of course about the notorious case of the Japanese fishermen in 1954 when their boat sailed through the fallout plume from an H bomb test at Bikini atoll and 23 men had to be treated for radiation sickness and one died. Black rain was part of the fallout here – and at the Hiroshima bombing at the end of the war. Joan was convinced that her husband was dead and so was Father and they soon all would be from the fallout. It took a while but Mother had some sherry in the house so a drink and a cup of tea calmed things down, by which time Bill came home and found the kids asleep in bed, no wife and came looking for her to take her off home calling her a 'Daft b****' as they left.

Father was in the control room again on another notable night, 14 October 1962 and this was when history was about to be made. There is no doubt that he was proud of his part in DFR - he had absolutely nothing to do with the first reactor on the site which was a test reactor but DFR was a UK first as an experimental fast reactor. He told Jon that it was the safest in the world and when Jon asked why he said because the fuel rods went into the reactor vertically and were held in place with magnetic clips. This was unlike cheaper American reactors, which had fuel rods that went in horizontally and were developed from reactors used on US submarines. If anything went wrong with the reactor said Father then the power to the clips would be cut and all the rods would drop through the reactor into a pit underneath, which would shut it down. That was not all, for the reactor was surrounded by a core made of graphite, and not all reactors had that; if the cooling system on this reactor failed then it would not overheat and melt like other reactors but would radiate the heat to the outside and keep running normally. Unlike other reactors the cooling was not done by water but by something else which just kept on going round even if the pumps were switched off. With a 10 year old's curiosity Jon asked that if these were so safe, why was there only one of them? Father said it was because they were far more expensive than normal reactors, and even though he thought the DFR a lot safer, he doubted many of them would be built because of the money and the big unsolved problem. What was that?

It was the waste.
Why was the waste a problem?
Well because it was highly radioactive.
So what did they do with it?
Well some was very low level waste and could be just buried and in a few years it would be quite safe, but a lot of it was highly radioactive and had to be treated differently.
Jon had not the faintest idea what radioactivity was except that it was dangerous in large doses.
So what did they do with that waste?
They turned it into ashtrays!
Ashtrays?
Father laughed and said that was what he and his colleagues called them. It seemed that the radioactive material was turned into brownish glass discs about the size of an ashtray and that in this form it could be stored.
Where could it be stored?
In a waste storage plant in a big pool of water.
Why water?
Because water was a very good shield against radioactivity.
Where were these pools?
Well they had one at Sellafield but they were talking of digging big caverns far under the ground or even under the sea to store the stuff.

Why could they not fire it into space and get rid of it? Jon had been reading about Dan Dare and Digby in the Eagle comic and space seemed a logical place to dispose of the waste.
Well because it would be very expensive and if there was an accident, radioactive waste would be spread all over the place - it was too risky.

Father clearly approved of nuclear power; it was cutting edge, the way to the future but he admitted freely in conversation that there was as yet no solution to the problem of what to do with the waste. He did come home absolutely hopping mad one day fuming about 'bloody fools' and spoke to mother about waste being put where it should not be put, but Jon was not really paying attention to him at that time.

So in October 1962 he was in the control room, doing his usual job and was standing by one of the panels waiting to flick a switch when told to do so. One of his bosses, came and said to him quietly;

'Alright Jack – we've got someone to do this bit.'

Father stood back and watched, as DFR became the first fast reactor in the world to supply electricity to a national grid - a landmark moment in scientific history and certainly a signal eyewitness moment. It seemed that the sky was the limit – Dounreay supported over 2,000 jobs, the town of Thurso had tripled from just over 3,000 to over 9,000 and the air was bright with hope, confidence and optimism. This was the United Kingdom Atomic Energy Authority's finest hour. It also seemed that Father's job was secure, his prospects for promotion were bright and that he and his family would be staying right where they were.

Later on, in 1962 Father decided that it was high time that Mother learned to drive – and indeed she wanted to. Driving at this time was far from a universal accomplishment and many men could not drive – Father had learned in the army, but Mother thought it a good idea that she drive so off they went to Dounreay. The old airfield was where many people learned to drive because its wide-open spaces and the fact that it was no longer used for aircraft at all, made it perfect for learners. Jon felt that was a shame and that it would make an excellent airport for Thurso, but the county airport was at Wick and two were not needed. In the huge expanses of the runways Mother learned to drive very quickly;

there was nothing to hit, plenty of space to manoevre and she swiftly became very competent. As he was confident in her, Father arranged a set of six lessons around Thurso to be followed by a driving test.

The morning of her test the roads were very icy but Father went with Mother down to the test centre and got out as her inspector got in. He was known as 'The Major' and was ex-army with a fine moustache and a reputation as a man of strong will. Mother wondered for a moment if he was old school and might have a problem with women driving but he told her to begin and sat back in his seat giving his instructions as they went off on the course round town, including an emergency stop on an icy road where the car skidded and mother controlled it. Forty-five minutes later they were back and a man came out of the test centre with a note.

'It's from Inverness – they phoned just after you left – there are to be no tests today because it's too icy.'
The Major pulled himself up and said;
'No tests today? Utter nonsense. There will be no more tests today, but they should have told me before I set off.'

Turning to mother he said;
'Congratulations Madam – you have passed with flying colours. Now if you will excuse me I will go and tell those idiots that there has been a test today and they WILL issue a letter to that effect. You may expect notification within a few days.'

The notification came. But Father still did most of the driving in the family.

The world did not end at Dounreay of course – there was plenty to the West of there, but to do it was serious exploration. Past Dounreay the modern A road petered out and became a very narrow single track road with passing places, very quickly threading its way not between fields but between vast seas of brown wind blown heather sweeping to the distance. Before that you could take a small lane down to Sandside Beach which was beautiful but they only went once. The Power Station was in full view of the beach and Father said that it was too much like a busman's holiday to go there - a constant reminder of work.

If Father's leisure could be defined it was as a motorist, as he took very little exercise but he did like to drive to see the area round the Far North. Out through Melvich, Strathy, Armadale and on to Bettyhill, Coldbackie and Tongue he would take the family, just for the pleasure of driving and seeing. Often this was in rain or mist and the trips were accompanied with Thermos flask, sandwiches of Shippam's paste, chocolate biscuits and apples. At Bettyhill Jon and Gill would have wished to stop but Father never did. As you came down the road there was one of the most glorious beaches imaginable, white gold with turquoise and aquamarine water, glistening on the edge of the land like a jewel in the sun. Father simply said that it was like any other beach, the water would be cold and they had a long way to go. The excursion usually turned round at Tongue because to go any further you had to go round an inlet of the sea that took you miles out of the way. Over the other side of the Kyle of Tongue you could see Achuvoldrach where the north coast road continued on its way but there was no bridge. On a couple of occasions the family did go further west to see Durness but that was as far as they got. Cape Wrath, its lighthouse and the great foghorns looking like giant Alpenhorns, would have to wait a long time if Jon was to see them.

Near Tongue was a road, which turned south and went up into the hills. Supposedly an A road, it did not look like one, still being narrow with the white diamond signs of passing places stretching into the distance. This was not to say that they were needed many times for in the next hour or so the family car met only one other vehicle. Quickly the terrain became mountainous and bleak uninhabited wilderness of heather, moor and peat. In the valleys were bushes and trees leant over by strong and frequent wind, but they did not catch the eye, for dominating the landscape were giant rounded hills with not a human nor a dwelling place in sight, and lochs twinkling blue in crisp clear air.

Jon looked at one huge and dominant pile and asked what it was called and was told that it was Ben Loyal and the loch in front, large, calm and without a boat or sail on it was Loch Loyal. Here in Hyperborean solitude was pantheistic wonder to rival anything in the world, a panorama so ravishing to the eye that had it been set in the heart of the Lake District, it would have been thronged with boats and people.

Searing savage beauty, wild, virgin and primitive was laid out before all comers for them to emboss in their inner minds as a mark against which to measure other places on earth. From here on Jon could listen to people speak of wonderful things across the world and think with inner certainty that they had not seen real beauty in nature until they saw the birds fly lonely over the grey waters of Loch Loyal in view of the Ben.

On then they went, down to Altnaharra to turn left up Strathnaver. The land here is tamer and greener with white farms and crofts dotted here and there, sheep and occasional cattle, still beautiful but nothing as feral as over the other side of the mountain. The road goes back up to the far north coast road and comes back onto it at Bettyhill unless you turn right at Syre and come home via Kinbrace and Strath Halladale, which the family did a few times. Once past Skelpick it runs close to the River Naver where is a good place to stop the car and have a sandwich and a drink. Often you have to do this with the window shut because the scourge of the Highlands, the thing that never appears in feature films, the plague that would defeat the best of Bravehearts, is out here in force. Culicoides Impunctatus or the Great Highland Midge swarms in clouds of dense black, biting and driving to screaming distraction anyone who is not protected against them. All over the Highlands they are found and are the curse of Hyperborea, but they are not fond of strong sunlight. If a child pleads enough, and the car is parked by a river, then that child may be allowed out to play and stretch his legs especially if the midges do not arrive. In this valley are low trees, shrubs, gorse bushes and bracken, which is quite thick. The ground is soft underfoot and if a boy should walk quietly and unintentionally down to the river without making a single sound then he might see something that he was not meant to see. In the flow of the river in the late afternoon sun, sitting on a mid stream boulder was a solitary otter and he had not seen Jon. The boy was hidden behind a gorse bush and the otter was looking into the water. For perhaps a minute the human stayed there motionless whilst the animal looked intently in front of him. Then without a splash he slid into the water and disappeared. Jon waited but he did not reappear so he ran back to the car and told everyone who then came rushing with excited noise – and of course saw nothing. It is worth getting out of the car and to those who think life's car is never worth getting out of to stroll down to the river, then think again.

104

This was not the first time that Jon had managed to glimpse those who would rather not be seen. Once on the road near Golspie he had been desperate for the toilet and had been for miles but Mother and Father did not stop and kept telling him that there was nowhere to go. Finally he blurted out that if they could not find him somewhere then he was going to have to do it in his pants. So reluctantly Father pulled the car over to the side of the A9 where there were bushes and Jon bounded out clutching some tissues. Just off the road and up a bank he dodged behind a bush and as he did so, its occupants decided that three was a crowd. The two fat deer in the bush did not hurry but moved off without stopping; nature in the Far North lives cheek by jowl with man though man may not see it. At the time though Jon did not care – he had other things on his mind.

One summer Father decided that he did not have enough money to afford a holiday to the south in Cumberland. There was a man at work who had a But and Ben out at Scourie in an idyllic setting and Father could have it for a week for 10 bob. Scourie was on the West coast of Sutherland, nearly at the top and it sounded good and Father booked his week right away. When the time came the family packed their holiday stuff, piled into the car and drove off along the North coast to Durness and turned South towards Scourie which was probably around 80 miles from home. Setting off early they arrived by lunchtime in a broad bay with a scattered village round it, bounded by hills and a clear sea inlet with a wonderful white beach. Jon and Gill could hardly wait. It is true that it was still the Far North of Scotland and that folk from the soft south would have found it still rather on the chilly side, but they were acclimatized by now and to them it was a warm summer day – they wanted to get into the water. They would have to wait though because they had to find their holiday home. This did not take long from the description the man at work had given Father on a piece of paper and there it was – a But and Ben about 100 yards from the water down a rough track which the car went down bumpily. Turning into a wide space between the house and an outbuilding, they parked in an overgrown yard in the middle of which sat an ancient car, windows missing and no wheels, which also had grass growing up through it and was dissolving into orange rust. The house was thatched and looked very old. The thatch was clearly ancient and in need of repair where it was rotting with patches of green moss growing on it and it was damp.

Inside was musty smelling and old; everything was old, from the faded carpet on the floor to the dark wood furniture and everything was slightly damp. Obviously it was not used much at all. Off to one side was the bedroom where Mother and Father would sleep and there was a low ceiling to the living room with a narrow ladder staircase up to a loft room with two single beds in it for Jon and Gill. Lying on the bed you looked straight up at the thatch and the rafters holding it up; there was no plastered ceiling as such. The dampness did not matter too much when it came to bedding because Mother had bought some cheap sleeping bags, which would be quite good enough for summer use.

So far was so good and after a sandwich lunch Jon and Gill clamoured to go to the sea and this was agreed. Changing quickly they dashed across the flat green sward between the house and the sea and straight into the water beside a rusty old iron pipe running into the water. Mother and Father followed; Mothers at on the grass by the shore and Father went in for a dip. The water felt great if chilly and it was very clear; seaweed, kelp and bladderwrack and dead man's fingers played round their feet and all was fine for a few minutes. Then Jon noticed a large lump of human poo floating in the water with some toilet paper at the same time as Father found what looked like a long white balloon floating in the water.

'Out – now!' he shouted. 'That's a sewage outlet,' and he pointed at the pipe.

The direct piping of raw sewage into the sea was a practice that was dying out, but still happened in remoter areas where there was no sewage farm or facilities yet for dealing with it. Father made them go back to the house and into a bath of clean water and also made them slosh their mouths out and gargle with salt water from a mug. It may or may not have worked, but they suffered no ill effects at all, or perhaps they simply had good immune systems from constant play and healthy constitutions. That, however, was the end of the sea bathing. The time was passed for the rest of the day with a walk, with ludo and then bed. Jon and Gill were tucked up warm in their sleeping bags up in the attic and being tired they both slept right through the night, which was just as well as it turned out. When they woke daylight was flooding into the attic skylight, and a new day beckoned.

It was decreed that they should visit Ullapool, which lay to the south but the day was dreich. It did not matter once in the warm and dry of the car so away to the south they drove until they came down to a short and steep hill down some trees and here the road ended. It was an A road indeed but there was a long inlet of the sea in the way at a place called Kylesku where a narrow part connected two lochs with Gaelic names. To get across you had to go onto the Maid of Kylesku, which was a two car ferry clanking across a chain to continue the road on the other side. A great advantage of it was that it was free. Though the weather was still slightly damp, down in the wooded valley where the dark water flowed through the channel, all was still. Jon saw that there was one more car in front of them and that the ferry was on the way back over towards them, clanking chain dripping as it came steadily over the gap. Father told them to all stay in the car, which was a disappointment as Jon wanted to get out and was sure that he would not fall into the icy deep water, but father was having none of it. In the car he and Gill stayed as the ferry clattered back over its route, heading for the small slipway, the grey shore of the other side and the low green trees looking so lush. Ullapool was a bit of a non event after that because they arrived, had fish and chips on the edge of the water, watched a big black and white ferry head back out to Stornoway and that was it. The weather did seem milder down here and Jon was quite surprised to see palm trees growing in some peoples' gardens. That, according to the oracle, was once again the effects of the Gulf Stream, that warm water current across the Atlantic washing along this coast, which meant that it did not freeze as much as it did further east in the winter. However, it did rain, and to say that Ullapool was a washout is a small understatement. Even the return trip via Kylesku seemed not as exciting as in the morning, but it was that night that was to bring the most interesting feature and rather a quick termination to the family holiday.

The evening was spent normally enough back at the But and Ben. Once the fire got going the faded damp carpet seemed to have dried out, the ancient damp smelling chairs were comfortable and the stone floor no longer cold. Ludo and reading were the order of the day, then Jon and Gill were told to go to bed. They did so and Mother and Father went into the downstairs bedroom shortly after. Upstairs Jon and Gill read for a while — she with her little comic and he with a book, as he had become a keen reader. Up above them the straw or hay of the thatched roof seemed cosy as outside a gentle rain fell; eventually Gill yawned and tucked herself down into her sleeping bag and was out like a light. Jon read a little longer, made sure his torch was in reach, then put the light out and went to sleep.

Unlike the previous night Jon woke up in the small hours. He needed to pee and the toilet was downstairs so he reached for his torch and clicked it on. Being drowsy from sleep he did not notice anything as he stepped out of bed and crunched towards the door.

Crunched.
Why crunched?

He looked down and woke up immediately. He could not see the carpet for a black mass and he was crunching through it in bare feet and it seemed to be alive because it was moving. There was no sense of alarm - Jon had never seen a horror film and had no feelings of fear but a rather intense curiosity so he reached out and switched on the light. Fear is often something that adults have had to learn and they fear things that children do not - nor have any reason to.

The floor was a black seething mass of tiny spiders so thick that they obscured the pattern in the carpet – how many there were he did not know – a million would perhaps be an understatement but you could not see the floor. It was a similar story when you looked up at the thatch. Gill was awake by now and wide-eyed at what she was looking at but strange as it may seem neither child was scared. It was odd but though the spiders covered the entire floor and much of the ceiling, they were not on the beds. Gill asked what they were doing and Jon said he did not know but he did not like it. There were a few big spiders up in the thatch but these mites on the floor all seemed miniscule, thick as a layer of sand and covering the floor of the room as far as you could see from wall to wall.

A voice from the stairs said 'What's going on up there?'
Father came up the stairs, opened the door and looked in the room.

The spiders did not like the light and were disappearing under the bed and back into the thatch, but he saw what was going on and he was quite decisive in what happened next.

'Right kids – clothes on now.'

They dressed while father shook out their sleeping bags just in case. He had already called down to mother, who was not fond of spiders at the best of times, to pack their stuff because they were leaving. Within 20 minutes they were packed, in the car and heading out with headlights blazing up the narrow road.

'Best thing to do with that dump' said Father 'is to burn it down!'

Whether or not Father got his money back after paying for a week but staying one and half nights, Jon never found out, but Father drove through the dark and by the time it was light they were on the outskirts of Thurso and soon after that, tucked up in their own beds, with no spiders at all.

This was not the family's only abortive holiday either. Father had to go to a meeting in Paisley in 1962 and he could have gone by train but chose not to. He decided to take some leave framed round his meeting, which would apparently be a short one, and make a sight seeing holiday of Central and Western Scotland. From somewhere he obtained the use of a pale blue Dormobile Camper van with a white top, which lifted up. As you lifted the top up a candy-striped canopy was also lifted up to make a sort of tent on top of the van. Two 'shelves' were then folded into place to form two bunk beds for children while the adults would sleep below in the main body of the van. This of course caused much excitement with Jon and Gill who had never been camping before and to whom it all seemed a wildly romantic thing to do.

The journey south was also not to be normal this time. They began by going West to Tongue then turning south down the A386 past Ben Loyal once again, but this time at Altnaharra they kept heading down towards Lairg a large village in Sutherland where four roads meet and which was sometimes called the 'crossroads of the Highlands.' This was new territory to explore and it did not disappoint. The road was single track again though with a good surface, and passing places stretched plentifully into the distance. The terrain was rolling hills and ridges covered with brown heather and rough grass, grey boulders and no trees whatsoever. Some of those would appear as they progressed on their way in the shape of Forestry Commission plantations of firs studding the landscape, but for the moment a few ragged bushes, stunted gorse and half-hearted bracken were the largest things actually growing. The most striking feature in the broadness of the high glen that the road followed for much of the time, was the complete lack of settlement and even of sheep; certainly it was not cattle country but there was enough of rough pasture for many sheep. The Highland Clearances of the 19th century had much of the blame for this because once in the valley floor there had been settlement, but now all was green wilderness.

After miles of this hard land the Crask Inn came as rather a shock because it came into sight and looked almost completely out of place. A large white painted house of two storeys and looking more like the local Manse, it sits solid in the land as a tiny cultivated island set in the wild with a cut lawn across the car-park area at the front.

If this were a true desert it would be an oasis, in the summer months at least, for here may be had tea and coffee, and in the moderate sized public bar of an evening a thirsty traveler may sink a beer and dine on the finest of venison stew before going up to well earned sleep in one of the comfortable bedrooms upstairs. Not for Jon and his family though; driving past with a glance they headed for Lairg with its stone houses, its streetlights, its pavements, roads and railway station at the bottom of clean cold Loch Shin, but there was no stop here either. This family had a favourite place to stop for a cuppa and it is a few miles further on across the Kyle of Sutherland by Bonar Bridge where the waters narrow and so to the Lady Ross at Ardgay. Soft and civilized is Ardgay, set in it valley with grass and trees, hunkering close down at sea level, mild and verdant. Now to see Angus!

The Lady Ross is a roadhouse, painted white and warm inside with a yellow glow of lights at night and they do chips and sausage and egg and sandwiches and anything else that a hungry traveler could wish for, but set up on a wall is the head of a stag with huge antlers and this is he whom Jon thinks of as Angus. His eyes are limpid and brown staring down full of sorrow and pity – and it is not surprising considering that he has been dead for many years. Jon liked Angus and thought it a great pity that he was dead and not roaming round the moors with his brothers and sisters. Father thinks this a little daft since Jon is quite fond of a piece of venison and says that he cannot have things both ways, which is quite correct. Saying goodbye to the stag and after visiting the loo, it is time for Struie so drive a few miles out of Ardgay and the road leaves the coast and goes up. Of course the main road is the one that stays low and goes round via Tain and Invergordon but that's a winter route. You can save miles if you cut straight over the moors of Strath Struie to Alness. It's beautiful up over the top where the wind blows all the fuzz from your head, and the colours of the purple heather, the lush green of the grass, and the starkness of the conifer plantations paint vivid pictures on the cortex of even the most liverish mind. Down to Dingwall, down the coast and across to Muir of Ord. It would be far, far quicker to do this bit if there were bridges across the sea inlets that cut into the coast, but they do not exist. Past Beauly to Inverness then down to the A9 and Aviemore. Aviemore, so Father says, is going to be a ski resort like Switzerland but Jon can't see it that way because it is so green and quite warm.

'Ah, but they get snow here in the winter,' said Father.
Every year?

Father could not answer that; Jon thought it was a nice looking little town but could not quite see it as a ski resort somehow. Now to King Gussie. Yes of course Jon knew it was Kingussie, but by now as well as the Beano and the Dandy he was occasionally reading the Topper and there was a character in the comic called King Gussie who lived in a castle with footmen, wore a crown and robes and had fairly normal neighbours and Jon just knew the artists had to have visited this small Highland town for their inspiration. On to Dalwhinnie, and thence to Blair Atholl. You must keep an eye open at Blair Atholl because once while passing through they saw a bunch of men in Highland uniforms and the children wondered why there were soldiers here. Mother it was who explained that they were Atholl Highlanders, and they were not part of the British army but belonged to the only private army in the country. That was all she knew about them but Jon quite liked the notion of having your own private army, and asked how many of them

111

there were. Father said there were about 30 of them but Jon did not think that was much of an army. If he had a private army then he would want one much bigger than that and would attack the Germans. That was apparently quite funny and Father said he read too many comics and warned him not to have a 'raging fury' like Captain Hurricane, the mighty marine from the Valiant who tore Germans apart every week in the comic.

Now they drove down the bloody pass of Killiecrankie and Jon knew well what had happened there where Bonnie Dundee had won the battle but been killed at the moment of victory. He peered round as they drove through, looking for bodies lying round but they had all gone. They must have cleared them up after the battle, which was a bit disappointing because he might have found a sword or a real gun to shoot people with. Feeling rather disappointed not to find a scene of carnage he asked where the bodies were and was told to shut up and not be a daft little bugger. That was the end of that speculation.

The dormobile puttered at last into Pitlochry, gateway to the Highlands and this was where it had been decided that they would stay the night. There was a campsite down by the river and there they stopped; it was lovely on a wide part of the river which some called a loch, under tall trees in a flat valley floor with the most beautiful green grass, cut like velvet. At first it was an idyll; Jon and Gill scampered round the site letting out all the pent up energy of the day shut in the van. Mother got dinner ready after Father had peeled the potatoes - a job that always had trousers on for some reason - and she seemed quite at home in the van with its small gas stove. Boiled potatoes with butter on, Spam, canned peas (Jon hated peas) and canned carrots, were followed by canned grapefruit with condensed milk – quite delicious.

Then came the bit where the roof was lifted and the shelves put into place for Jon and Gill to sleep on. Into their sleeping bags they went with the metal of the roof above their heads, the candy stripe waterproof fabric next to them, and the skylight open a bit to ventilate the space. Both children stayed in bed all night so there was no bother about getting out; Jon woke up at some point and felt cold but he tucked his head down into his bag and breathed into instead of outside his bedding.

That seemed to work better than having his head outside for it warmed things up a bit and he went back to sleep.

When he woke up in the cold dawn light Mother was in a foul temper and it lasted all morning. She had not slept a wink - she was frozen stiff. She hated camping and if Father thought she was going to spend another night in that uncomfortable bed then he had another think coming. Oh dear. The children did not agree with it but dare not open their mouths, because there was a distinct likelihood that they would have been answered with the flat of her hand. After breakfast the journey continued in a sort of sour silence of the sort that mother knew well how to deliver.

They slowed down as they always did when driving through Stirling — the traffic there was perpetually nose to tail on the main North Road the great highlight being the garage that you went past that had a real car mounted on the wall above the main door. Jon thought that was quite groovy and that it was a racing car, though he was not sure.

Glasgow was interesting though the children were not sure about it. Father had said that there were some rough people living there and Jon knew from his friends at school who came from some place called Gorbals, that there were gangs there who used knives and they had lot of fights. There were interesting things to see though, but what really caught the attention was the public transport. As the dormobile drove through the city Jon shouted out; 'Look – trams!'

Sure enough there were two trams passing each other painted orange, green and cream, running along real lines set in the road. They were full of people and Jon, who had never seen such a thing before, longed to have a go on one of them. Father said that there was not time and they must get on to Paisley because he would have to find somewhere to stay the night. He also said that Jon should take good of looking at the trams because they would not be there for much longer as they were going to get rid of them. To the boy that seemed a very silly thing to do and he asked why. The answer was that they were dangerous and that they caused accidents. When pressed on how they caused accidents Father said that people riding bikes caught their wheels in the tracks and fell off hurting themselves. He might have been speaking from

113

experience though he did not say, but Jon got the impression that he really was not fond of trams, and especially when he added that they were old fashioned and inefficient, and that buses were better.

In Glasgow the buses were also like no others that Jon had seen because they had great arms sticking out of the top that touched overhead wires. They also were green orange and cream and there were a lot more of them than trams. They only saw the two trams but the trolleybuses were everywhere and a fascinating thing was when the arms at the top ran over a bad place in the overhead wires and there was a bright flash so that you wanted to watch them to see if they did it again. Father found a side street and parked the van; he then told Gill and Jon that they had to stay in the van, which he would lock; he and mother were going to go off to find some grub. It being lunchtime this sounded a good idea so Gill and Jon settled down into the Dormobile seats and read their comics. They ignored the people passing on the pavement outside because the truth was that they were both a little worried about being left on their own in a place where Father had said that there were rough people. However within five minutes Mother came back with a white cardboard box, which she upended on the surface by the sink and lifted off to leave four large pink conical iced cakes with a knob of cream on top of each, sitting on a square of cardboard.

'That's for dessert,' she said and appeared to be in a much better mood than she had been all day.

'Don't touch them and make sure they don't get knocked over.'
Then she left again, locking the van and went off to find Father who was doing some shopping out of sight.

Jon and Gill looked even more apprehensively out through the window. The cakes were in plain sight of all the people passing on the pavement – what if they wanted to take them? A man came along the pavement wearing a flat cap and in a long raincoat and saw the cakes and the two children. He looked at them, then at the cakes, smiled and licked his lips.

'Nooooooooo!' they both shouted and jumped forward both putting their arms protectively round the cakes.

The man laughed like a hyena, not in any nasty way at all, and walked off about his business. Mother and Father came back very soon with sandwiches and drinks and crisps and Mother was quite back to normal. Father had decided that he could afford bed and breakfast that night in Paisley and there would be no need to camp, which greatly disappointed Jon and Gill but cheered Mother up no end.

What do you do in the prosperous mill town of Paisley if you do not wish to spend the entire evening in bed and breakfast in 1962? Why, you go to the Regal Cinema because they are showing Pinnochio. Even better, as the family took their seats in the cinema they were playing Telstar by the Tornadoes, which was brilliant because all the kids at school thought they were cool. Popcorn, the innocent Pinnochio, the bad wolf, Jimmy Cricket and the film itself which is probably the best Disney Cartoon of all; and of course its moral message is as plain and true as it ever was - don't tell lies!

Next morning was dreich and dismal and the children had to sit with their mother in a car-park for over two hours while Father went into a meeting at a red brick modern building just across the road. When he came out it was time to head for home since Mother had taken against camping and they certainly could not afford to do bed and breakfast again. In the puttering Dormobile, which did not go very fast, this would take the rest of the day so without delay they set off from Paisley, back through Glasgow. As they drove, Jon could hear Mother and Father talking in the front seats about a place called Hunterston but he 'did not think that he had got it'.

The gist of it was that Father had been after a considerable promotion and a lot more pay, but was not successful. The boy might have felt the earth move at that moment, but since Father had not got the job, it stayed stable. Soon the Dormobile came to traffic lights and road works and had to follow a diversion round some back roads and in between some rolling hills. Everywhere they looked there were buildings going up on what had been open fields, and in places it still was fields. Jon asked where they were, struck by the scale of the operation; he had obviously seen large building sites round the schemes in Thurso, but this was on a scale altogether much bigger. Father said that they were in a place called Cumbernauld and that the government had decided to build a new town there. Why? Well because there were so many people living in Glasgow and many of them lived in bad housing called slums and that these were so that they could move out and improve how they lived with better homes and more space. Jon did not like the look of Cumbernauld and thought that the new houses and blocks were grey and dull, looking like shoeboxes with sloping lids just scattered over the hills. Of course it was raining and the drab concrete with which the houses were all rendered was dark and dingy with the soaking of it, but Mother said that she would not wish to live in such a place. It was a concrete rabbit warren and she did not care if she never saw it again — she also pitied the people who would have to live there.

When they got home it was dark and time for bed; Jon went to bed glad to be back where he belonged. This was his place – not just the house, but the town, the river, the beach, the people. Hyperborea was his and he lived in it as a fish swims in water.

Would that things were always so!

Then There Were Three

To a child, big people are big and really that is all there is to it. Mother never looked particularly large or fat until Jon was older and he actually thought about it. To an adult in 1960 she probably looked quite young and slim and indeed she was not yet 30 so in all likelihood, she was. Perhaps she might have put on weight over Christmas 1960, but if she did neither Jon nor Gill noticed. He was eight years old and would very quickly be nine and he had just been given a Triang train set, which engaged all his attention. He set it out in the living room with Father's assistance and connected it up to a big transformer that looked, to his mind, like a wedge of black cheese covered in hard metal paint and had a large knob in the front labelled AC if you turned it one way and DC if you turned it the other. Father did tell him about alternating and direct current but he did not understand a word of it. All he knew was that if you turned the knob one way the train went forward and if you turned it the other it went backwards.

Mother had her fit at about 3.20pm on Christmas Day - this was normal. The time varied, but the children used to wait for it to happen, for they knew it would. Every Christmas Day it was the same; Mother would be cheerful, happy and all Christmassy - but at some point in the afternoon the mood would change. The air would become sour and Mother would take offence at something someone had done. Who it was varied but it was usually Jon or Gill – rarely Father though that was not unknown. You could never tell what was going to bring it on so it was difficult to avoid; after the family acquired a television the subject matter was often what channel it should be on. Part of the problem was that when Mother got upset she would appeal to Father, and they being much of a unit, he would back her up, no matter what, and no matter how unjust. This year Gill had done something, but afterwards neither of them could quite remember what it was she had done. Mother flew into tears and demanded of Father if he was going to allow HIS daughter to speak to her like that. Gill knew he was going to slap her so she fled into the kitchen. Father chased after her with his hand raised, but so did Jon who was absolutely aflame. Even at eight he had a fairly developed sense of injustice and as Father lifted his hand Jon flung himself in front of his sister who was five and shouted, fists clenched in the air; 'Leave her alone – she's done nothing!'

117

So Father hit him instead. He did not hit back but stood there as Father shouted at him to get out of the way. He did not, so Father slapped him again. All Jon did was raise his fists up and glare but he did not hit Father, though he wanted to. He was not doing what was right.

Father stopped and told them both to go to their rooms – but they went to Gill's room where they hugged each other and dissolved into tears.

Do not wonder, reader that things should be this way because that is how it was. Parents were strict and used violence freely to enforce their will, strong in the belief that they would keep their children in righteous ways by doing so. It was accounted good parenting. It may be that you wonder at having this tale related, but the author has no compunction over doing so; it happened, and it needs to be written for it is a cautionary tale. Be in no doubt that if you beat your children to keep them humble and obedient, then you set a line between them and yourself. They will know that your love for them is conditional and they must behave in particular ways. This lesson, once learned, is never forgotten and it never goes away. Your children will never come to you for hugs; you will never be close to them. They will not tell you of their troubles and you will always have set a line of reserve between you and them, for you have ruled them by fear - and fear is never lost, never forgotten. It might be understood, and it might, in due time, be forgiven but the consequences of it, in the long run, may fester and turn to bad ways and it is, in brief, never worth the short term obedience that the fear you inspire brings about.

When the temper had subsided, and the mood had passed Jon and Gill were told to come downstairs for Christmas tea and no more would be mentioned of what had passed, even if Jon thought that Father looked slightly sheepish and that Father and Mother both tried very hard to be nice. It was perhaps a good time to be told that they were going to have a new brother or sister and that he or she would be arriving in February.

How this was going to happen was quite clear. In answer to where babies come from, Mother said that they were found under gooseberry bushes. This caused some momentary consideration by Jon and Gill. Jon found the answer – was it the gooseberry bush on the A882 (now

A9) just up the hill from the bridge on the way to Wick? In a more cynical and worldly age it would no doubt be thought laughable that a boy of eight was so ignorant of the facts of life, but in this period, children were not told such things. It may be that they were allowed to be children for far longer than at other times in history but Jon read comics, a strictly censored television still inspired by Reithian rigour, and his teachers were not expected to tell him things at school that his parents had on their job description from immemorial time. After all it was not long before this that people were able to get married without knowing the facts of life; one could be imprisoned for being homosexual, and if a woman had a child out of wedlock she was still regarded as being stigmatised and disgraced. What chance did Jon have? If Mother said that babies were found under gooseberry bushes, then some strange process of nature that he did not understand put them there and that was that.

One day in February 1961 Mother told Jon and Gill that the baby was going to come and that they must stay downstairs out of the way - she was in the bedroom with Father. Dr Giddis popped in at some point during the afternoon, went upstairs and stayed for a while then he left. Then a lady nurse in a dark blue uniform pulled up out front in her car and got out carrying a large black bag. Jon and Gill exchanged glances meaningfully – the baby was in that bag! As the nurse came through Gill breathed;

'Is it a boy or a girl?'

This question was obviously very important to her. The District Midwife nurse smiled and said that they would have to wait and see and went upstairs to see Mother. Afternoon went on, and the evening and hours had gone by. Occasionally there was some noise from upstairs and the children thought it was taking an awful long time to get this baby started up. Eventually Doctor Giddis came back to the house and also trotted upstairs, but with all that he could do it was still quite late when Jon and Gill heard a loud 'Waaaaaaaah' from upstairs and knew that there was a new member of their family. Eventually it seemed that everyone upstairs was happy because the Doctor left with a smile and a pat on the head for Gill, and shortly after that, the nurse. Father then told them that they could come up and see the new baby so they ran

119

upstairs to see Mother sitting up in bed with a scrunch-faced figure wrapped up and cradled in her arm.

'What is it?' said Jon?
'Say hello to your baby sister,' said Mother.
'Hello,' said Jon kneeling down to get a closer look.
'Take it back – we don't want it.' said Gill, bursting into tears. 'We don't need it – take it away!'

Gill changed in that moment and not in a small way. Her entire status in the family had shifted. One minute before she had been the girl, the baby of the family, cosseted and fussed over. Now, within seconds, not only was she that potentially problematic figure, a middle child, but she was no longer her Father's little girl because there was another one smaller and her life would never be the same again. Perhaps some compensatory behaviour, some notion of reassurance would have helped her, but these ideas were not common currency and her parents just laughed and thought that her nose was temporarily out of joint and that she would get over it in a few days. In such times are our moods coloured and our tempers set, so they were wrong and from the trauma of this event, the perceived displacement of parental affection and her own ranking, however misguided, Gill was never quite the same again.

Next day Jon was outside playing on the front lawn of number 6 with Susie from over the road and announced that he had a new sister that the nurse had brought in a bag from a gooseberry bush. This girl was rather more learned than he and told him that babies came out of Mummy's tummys. Jon thought this not true and scoffed loudly asking that if it was true, then how did they get there? Susie said that her Daddy had told her that babies got into Mummy's tummy because he put a seed in there where it grew into a baby. When Jon pursued this line of thought, asking where her Daddy got the seed from and how he put it there, Susie's knowledge dried up for she simply did not know any more. The matter was soon forgotten in his mind and it was to be another couple of years before he learned the true facts of life in the way that many if not most boys heard them in those days; in smutty prurient rumours, half-whispers and dirty jokes passed round by small boys in school. A strange omission in a civilised society that does not teach its children the basic facts of reproduction then wonders in later life at the smutty and sexist attitudes some men have towards women. It's simple - if ignorance is left to see the opposite sex, in a child's formative years, as the objects of dirty jokes, of innuendo, as things for sexual gratification and as 'other' then that is the future structure of society. Better to let the light of day shine on such things and educate children properly in what they need to know. Jon was an innocent, an ignoramus, and naïve – and he was far from being alone among his fellows in this.

Over the course of the next few days Mother and Father ummed and awed about what to call the baby and finally settled on Valerie, known to one and all as Val and indeed that was her own preference. As she grew and learned eventually to talk, she said her own name 'Walawi' but it soon became 'Wal'. Jon pushed her around in her pram and of course she was watched very carefully the whole time.

The baby's head had to be wet of course and she was duly christened in the Episcopalian Church, High or not. The priest might have thought Mother would return to worship there if he christened Val but she did not. Ron and Ivy Dodds, the nice couple who lived in the semi attached to number 6 were named as Godparents, but it was a task they were never called upon to fulfil. The night of the christening Mother and Father had a party. The baby was in her cot upstairs and various grown-ups from all over Thurso trooped in the have a dram and dips and snacks. Mother had devised a dip from a sachet of dried tomato soup and tomato sauce, mixed with some salad cream that she got from a book. It actually tasted nice and Jon and Gill were allowed to dip crisps in it to try – and wanted more. Mother said that it was quite the hit at the party, but Jon and Gill were not there. They were, in theory, in their rooms asleep. In fact they were wide awake and hanging over the banister rail upstairs hoping to be invited down because the adults were having a very good time of it. Father, who did not usually like people in his house, being quite a shy man, had moved the furniture back. Mother's little record player was belting out dance music and there appeared to be quite a hop going on down there.

The tune of the evening was Zambesi by Lou Busch which had been released in 1956 and which was a catchy band number calculated to get feet tapping – it was definitely not pop because Mother and Father both sneered at stuff like the Shadows and the Tornadoes, preferring big

121

bands. Joe Loss and Skyliner featured too, with some Glenn Miller, which was Mother's absolute favourite; so did Frank Sinatra, but Zambesi was repeated at least six times during the evening. Be that as it may, the infant prodigy's head was well and truly whetted and both parents rose late the next morning with some tidying up to do. Time to be parents for a new Val.

Val had a mind of her own and it showed more and more as she grew and it was this that led to an experiment of a most unfortunate type.

On 4 April 1962 Jon and Gill were outside number 6 playing and a whole cloud of neighbourhood kids were there too. The radio was on inside and loud; since it was quite warm the front window was open too. The man on the radio announced that the murderer James Hanratty had been hanged that day; Jon did not know anything at all about this man, but if he had murdered someone then he hanged – that's what happened to you if you murdered people. Mother was in the kitchen and Val was supposed to be in the house - only she was not. A precocious toddler she had wandered out of the kitchen, down the hall and out of the front door. She had then come down the front step and felt hungry. Hidden in the grass of the lawn were several of the large black and shiny slugs that are common in Hyperborea. What she saw them as may only be conjectured, but when Jon turned round and saw her a picture of her embossed itself onto his memory with half a slug in her hand. The other half was in her mouth and she was chewing very carefully with a most thoughtful look on her face.

'Mother – Val's eating a slug!' yelled Jon.

Mother came flying out of the house, knocking the slug out of Val's hand and then prying her mouth open to hook out what she was chewing. Then she picked her up and took her indoors and set her lying on the draining board with her head over the sink while she washed her mouth out with carbolic soap. Val did not like this process one little bit and there were loud yells and screams - the taste of soap was not one she appreciated. Eventually Mother finished cleaning her mouth out, rinsed her repeatedly and told her never to eat slugs again. The little girl did not say anything, as she did not talk much yet. She made up for it later, when she could talk fluently and still remember the slug and she told Jon that it had tasted bad. She would not be eating any more of them.

The baby's special delight was the car; at first she sat on Mother's lap on family excursions, but later she graduated to sitting in the middle of the back seat between Gill and Jon. Gill, in the worst throes of sibling rivalry, did not like this at all and used to elbow the smaller girl over out of 'her' space. Val was too young to comprehend jealousy, but used to jump up and down smiling broadly as the car went along yelling; 'Tuk-a-tuk car! Tuk-a-tuk car!'

This continued for months and it was quite plain that Mother did not just have a daughter but a motorist, whose liking for cars was hard-wired in right from the start.

Thus, two children were now three and strange to tell, the new baby, born a Scot, also liked the bagpipes and also went to sleep to the Rowan Tree, much to Dr Giddis's disgust. When watching the Thurso pipeband the baby flew into raptures, waving at the pipers from her pram and gurgling strange noises as they went past.

During June it was almost as entertaining to watch Val's reactions during the Gala Parade as it was to watch the Gala itself. The Gala Week was a festival of all sorts of events and competitions, which culminated in a parade and the crowning of a Gala Queen.

On the Saturday morning the banks of the river down by the harbour were crowded with folk on both sides – even over by the castle where Jon never went. Father said that there were to be hi-jinks on the water whatever they were, but Jon soon found out. There were races between groups of men who had built rafts out of all sorts of things, dressed in just about anything they pleased it seemed. Lots of splashing went on and folk got knocked into the water quite a lot. Another race was between boats and Jon thought it might be serious until he saw that there were about 20 boats and that they were not for racing but were from the boating pond up at the mill. They were rowed by one person, each in a different costume – some Vikings and some pirates and they raced upstream to above the Ellan Foot-Bridge which was thronged with people, then at a signal each man turned this boat round to face downstream, stopped rowing and reached down to take up the wooden flooring from the bottom of the boat and held it up as a sail to catch the wind. The crowd thought this hilarious and gales of laughter swept across the river. Then there was a duck race but Mother did not want to stay to watch any more for she was cold and wanted a cup of tea. They could all come back later for the parade.

The whole centre of the town was decked out in flags for a high bright sunny day and the shops were closed as for a holiday, which indeed it was. The Gala route was from the wide street on the other side of the river along by the egg warehouse, then over the bridge and up to Sir John's Square, along Traill Street, round Olrig Street and back along Princes Street.

Led by the pipe band marching impassively and impressively to Terribus, up past the cinema to turn right by Hamish Cameron's, the floats would begin and the sights would be seen - and what sights. All sorts of strange and fantastical costumes of a variety spanning the imagination and ingenuity of man could be seen. Scarecrows and sheikhs, witches, wizards, Africans, Indians and Turks, Red Indians, tramps, kings and yokels all trooped past or leered off slow moving floats or lorry backs, waving charity collecting tins. Health and Safety was a thing unknown as young men, bashi-bazouks, Foreign Legionaries and Tudor courtiers stood unsecured on the top of the cabs of moving lorries, supporting each other. Other marching bands also took part – there was the Salvation Army band and a detachment of Boy's Brigade; there were sea scouts and brownies, fishermen and emperors. Such a show as was never seen and in the middle a float with the glittering Queen in a white dress with two attendant goddesses eventually heading for her ceremonial coronation in the park in the middle of Sir John's Square. Peering past the bronze war memorial, leaning his hand on 'Heddle' on the plaque, Jon could see a man put the crown on her head but he did not know who he was except that he looked important. Momentarily he was confused and wondered aloud if it was the real Queen but Mother told him not to be so daft. Home then, to dinner and to more indifferent things and life as it is.

Speaking of the Boys' Brigade was what confused Mother and provided a classic example of misinformation that led to an object lesson in how

124

to get rid of Mormons. This is not to say anything against Mormons but Mother was C of E and had no time for them. When two well barbered Americans turned up at the house one Sunday morning it was Mother who answered, cradling Val in her arms and instead of telling them that she was not interested, engaged in religious disputation with them. She had a habit though of getting only part of the information she needed and using it anyway, like bullets. To Mother the world was a place full of people who were out to get you and you got on in life by scoring them off. It might have been easy to blame the Daily Record, the Sunday Post or the Daily Express for framing such a view, but her upbringing had not been an easy one. She would use any ammunition she could grab hold of and would never admit to being wrong in anything. In this case she ended the discussion by chiding them that if they were in the UK and in Thurso they should not be keeping her on the doorstep on Sunday morning but should have a quiet reflection at the birthplace of their founder which was at Janetstown, just outside Thurso. The Mormons exchanged mystified glances upon which Mother explained in a superior manner that Joseph Smith, the founder of the Mormon religion, was born nearby and she would not waste their time any more – they should go and have a look.

'Well thank you Ma'am. We did not know that but you may be sure that we will go and have a look.'

Presumably they did so, but they would have been disappointed. There are an awful lot of Smiths in the world, easy to get mixed up with, and William Smith, founder of the Boys Brigade, was not born at Janetstown but at Pennyland House, which was just along the road from number 6. In this respect Janetstown was entirely guiltless.

The family car was in trouble. The Morris 1000 traveller was an excellent car with lots of space for the children and they really liked it – but it stood outside in all weathers and it had wooden framework for the back part. The wood had started to rot rather badly and Father could not afford to have it repaired. He scanned the Exchange and Mart and eventually found something very tempting, which he should have reflected upon – but did not for he was sometimes impulsive. Someone down in Forres, Morayshire, was selling a Wolseley 6/80. This was the sort of car used by the Police in the 1950s, but this one was privately owned and Father's mouth watered. He had to have it. The seller was a doctor and therefore a man of good reputation who could be trusted. Father phoned him and heard that the car was excellent in all ways and so he clinched the deal. He would go to Forres on the train and bring cash and drive back. To Jon's pleasure Father decided he wanted company on the journey and took Jon with him. Four hours down from Thurso to Invernecky as Father insisted on calling Inverness in a steam train with compartments. Clickety clack, clickety clack was what Jon recalled ever after. The journey seemed never to end and would have been quicker by car he thought. And then there was another train out to Forres where Father handed over the money and took possession of his prize. It was absolutely beautiful - shiny black with a walnut dashboard, leather seats and easily the poshest car that Jon had ever seen. To his eyes it looked like a Rolls Royce. Father took the wheel and they drove back in pride to Thurso. By the time they got there Father was muttering about tappets - and as it turned out he had bought yet another mechanical pig whose bonnet he was for ever tinkering under. There is a reason you get things cheap and another why you beat all the other people who might wish to buy something. Father liked cars. This was a nice car and he saw no further. For a short time, a few months this was the family's transport and quite undeservedly, it did turn heads. It looked what it was not.

Mother's mood was greatly lightened one day in late 1962 when her son, now nine years old, announced that he would cook dinner. Although she found this amusing at first, the temptation was too much and she said that this was fine – she and Father and Gill and Val would go for a walk and looked forward to dinner when they got back. Accordingly, as they set off for a nice stroll down to Victoria Walk, looking out over the sublime scenery of a sunny Thurso Bay at 10.00am, Jon put a chicken into the electric oven in number 6. He had seen mother do this many times and it was simple. He peeled and parboiled potatoes and at 11.30 am he put those in the oven too. Carrots, cabbage and neeps were also done – and Jon knew how to make gravy. Roasts really are rather simple.

Now it was time for the *piece de resistance* and Mother was not expecting this at all. Jon had decided to show off a little and he mixed up a sponge mixture, spooned jam into a steaming bowl and carefully

126

poured the sponge mix on top. Then into the steamer it went to cook while he made a pan of custard.

Reader, it is an easy thing to do but reflect that he was nine years old and had never cooked a full dinner in his life. All was done well, the family returned and sat down to Sunday dinner followed by a light sponge topped with hot jam and custard - it was delicious. Then for the tidying up; Jon had done much of the washing as he went along but the surfaces were rather covered in bits and Jon, in a hurry, swept them onto the floor.

That did it. Mother, who had been praising the chicken, the sponge, the custard, now called him a dirty little beast for sweeping the crumbs onto the floor and all turned to sackcloth and ashes, all achievement swept away and nullified by this one absent act. Perhaps the kitchen was her domain; perhaps she did not wish him getting above himself, but the balloon of what he had done was pricked and burst as he retreated to his room profoundly upset. It is a mark of her achievement that though he was perfectly able to cook, he never offered to do so again.

He peeled vegetables - that was his job. He dusted, did the vacuum cleaning and whatever tasks he was told to, but the next meal he cooked was not to be for many years. Parent - if you praise your child for its achievements and bring out a pride and a confidence in its abilities, do not then destroy the accomplishment with a small word, because then they will not wish to achieve for you. If you do not try then you cannot fail; therefore praise your child justly in what he or she does, and let it stand. So it is that you will build confident and well-adjusted beings who are a credit to you. Otherwise you will get a lackey who does as he or she is told – and that is all. What have you gained? If you learn nothing else from reading these lines then remember this.

On day outside Hamish Cameron's shop, Jon saw a black person. Mother was behind him with Val in a pram, and round the corner came someone who was not white, which caught him upon the instant, for he had never seen anyone who was not white before though he had seen pictures in books. It has to be said that he gaped and stared and the man looked right back at him with an expression that was mildly amused; it may be supposed he appeared to be used to such attention from small and ignorant white boys.

'Owwwwwww!'
Mother was furious and had just fetched him a slap on his ear.
'It's bad manners to stare at people! How many times do I have to tell you that? It's rude!'
And with that she slapped the other ear.

The man had walked on by with a sympathetic look at Jon, but had said nothing. The message was clear enough. Staring at people was rude. Staring at people because they were a different colour was rude. Do not stare at people because of the colour of their skin – there may well be reasons for staring at them for other things, but this is not one of them. It might be a valid speculation to ponder on how much racism in the world could be nipped in the bud at an early age by a clip on the lughole.

One of Jon's ears is slightly bigger than the other, but his manners were reasonably civilised.

Val's arrival on the scene focused Father's attention on where they lived; number 6 had four bedrooms it is true, but they were small and the house was hard to heat with no central heating and expensive electric fires in every room. He took a walk on his own up to Mount Vernon, which was the other side of the river on the hill, and there were virgin fields where houses were a building, right up to the wall of the town cemetery; a new estate. These houses were different. Although they were semi-detached like number 6, they were larger, with an attached garage, and central heating. The central heating was rather different though – it was not through radiators but was quite revolutionary in Jon's eyes – warm air came up out of ducts in the floor at the side of each room; truly this was modernity. A new baby probably placed Father at some advantage in his negotiations as infants play well in the minds of those empowered to consider such things, but Father put his name down for one of the new houses and his efforts were rewarded by being allocated the best house in the whole town.

To any who doubt the veracity of this statement there is a remedy. Take a walk up to Mount Vernon and go into number 1. It sits at the entrance to a road, and on the very edge of the estate – but it is where it is that determines its excellence. In front of the house is a small triangle of grass bounded by new laid pavement, and a low slab wall between this and a steep field sloping down into the valley. The view from this position is wonderful, especially if you can enter the house and go into the front bedroom. From this eminence you may see laid before you the whole valley, looking down towards the harbour, out to sea, and in the far, far distance may be seen the Old Man of Hoy. If you can stand at that view and not feel a pricking in the eyes at the sheer elemental and ferocious beauty of it, then you need a stiff dose of human feeling, for it is unrivalled. From here on a clear night in late autumn you may see the Heavenly Dancers in the sky, which is, to Hyperboreans, a special bonus of living here. The great shifting colours of the Aurora Borealis moving round the vault of blackness round God's great firework display, may be taken for granted by the child who lives up there all the time, but the sight is one that never fades. Jon saw the Northern Lights more than once in his life and thought it part of the scenery – the normal run of life. Father of course explained all about particles reacting as they hit the atmosphere over the top of the world, but to Jon they were wonderful enough at first, though exposure to them brought familiarity and from his house he had a ringside seat. Were it in some millionaire paradise in a warmer clime, rich men would fight for the privilege of that view; all Jon had to do was to look out of the living room window.

In early October 1962 the family packed all their worldly goods and moved house, across the river, leaving number 6, home for four years, and moved to number 1. This then was to be their future home - if they survived. A few days after they moved in, Father turned on the television news and got very grave indeed. There on the screen Jon watched a black and white picture show what seemed to be a very frightening story. It was a strange thing to lie on the floor of number 1 with warm air gushing out of the metal vents in the floor and watch a line of American destroyers blockading Cuba. Father was very worried – and so therefore was Jon. It appeared that the Americans and the Russians were going to start fighting and this would mean World War 3. It could actually be the end of the world because they would use nuclear bombs and everyone would die. Thurso would be a target because of

129

Dounreay and the Russians would wish to destroy it because if was a nuclear station and made stuff that could be used to make nuclear bombs. In the end though the Americans won, as they always win, so everyone could relax.

There was, however, a massacre, which was to have a long lasting effect and it concerned Teddy, Snowball and Panda. Teddy was Jon's bear whom he had cuddled since he was born, bought out of Gus Risman's shop in Workington - a retired rugby player who opened a sports and toy shop when he quit the game. Gill had many dolls and soft toys but doted on Panda, so named for obvious reasons and more especially Snowball, a white fluffy bear with bright blue eyes. The children played with these together and they usually lived in Gill's toy pram and this was kept in the garage that adjoined the house.

One day Mother announced that she was throwing them all out. She stated that they were damp and mouldy and should not have been left out in the garage, so because they were mildewed they were unhealthy and they were going in the bin. There was the most tremendous and dramatic scene in the kitchen with Gill doing her little nut, Jon doing his and Mother doing hers, but Mother threw the lot in the bin. The mental distress was appalling to both children and Jon set his face into a mask of determination, marched to the bin, pulled Teddy out and pushed his way past Mother up to his room. He kept his bear. Snowball, Panda and all the other soft toys in the pram went and Mother had her way with them.

The strange thing was that noone followed Jon or questioned where the bear was, and he kept him, old, scuffed of most of his fluff and with one eye, and he wondered if Mother had actually consulted Father at all about throwing the toys out. Perhaps she had not, but Gill, who was feeling displaced anyway by the arrival of another girl, was most injured and hurt. From this time on, things were never the same between Mother and Gill as they had been. If you tyrannise children and commit outrage upon their prized possessions, then beware, for the reward you reap for your short-lived triumph may be a long and bitter harvest.

Jon was rather bored. He had been sorry to leave number 6 because he had friends there. It is true that if he got off his backside and went out these friends were just a 15 minute walk away across the footbridge, along the river path, up Lover's Lane and then onto Castlegreen Road, but it was not the same as going to Susie's door and knocking, or Jan and Mike's. As yet, in the new house and in the immediate vicinity, he had no friends and the house next door was still empty. Besides which, it was cold. The winter was coming on and although there was no snow, there were hard frosts. Jon was going to school well muffled up; slides were being made on the hard frost of the playground during morning break. He was staying in the house a lot, reading and watching the telly. His life was about to change, though he did not know it, and the change would not take effect for over a year. In December of 1962 school was about to break up for Christmas but Mother did not care two hoots about that. On Sunday 9 December 1962 Gill and Jon had just got up and were sitting on the floor of number 1. Val was toddling about the other side of the room, occasionally warming her bottom by plonking it down on one of the warm air vents. Mother was ironing with the red and cream iron she had received for a wedding present, at the wooden ironing board with the asbestos plate for the iron. Father was in the garage soldering something, as he often did.

Suddenly Mother said;
'Do you want to go to Mam's for Christmas?'

Both the older children liked their grandparents Mam and Dad immensely. Of course they did. The response was immediate and seemed spontaneous. Mother put down the ironing, switched the iron off, put it away and went to see Father. Within the hour they were gone, in the Wolseley and heading south.

South

This was not the first time that the family had travelled the long way south to see Mam and Dad in the time that they had lived in the Far North. In the winter of 1960 Father and Mother decided to go with the children to visit relatives back where they used to live in Cumberland for Christmas. They travelled down by train, which was slow and expensive. The journey down from Thurso to Inverness took four hours and by the time they got there it was lunchtime. Luckily there was a rather large station restaurant and father said that they could have anything they wanted. On the door was a picture of a black bull whose name was Aberdeen Angus and the steaks were supposed to be delicious. Jon wanted one of those with chips but Gill preferred fish. When his steak arrived he was asking Father what mustard was for and Father said with a smile that it was for putting on your steak. Although he was not sure what Father was smiling for the boy decided to put some on his steak and then bit into a fork full. It was so hot and the heat of it went up his nose and brought water to his eyes as he gasped and drank some of his lemonade to cool it down. Father thought it was funny but his son, who had a bloody streak to his nature, was not going to allow this to be the finale to the scene. He ate the rest of the steak, with the mustard, and by the end of it he was enjoying it - he liked steak with mustard. From then on he asked for mustard with his meat at every opportunity and had developed a growing taste for strong flavours. Father's little joke had turned a definite corner in his son's preferences and at age seven he was developing his lifestyle tastes.

Mam and Dad at this time owned and ran a fish and chip shop in Brook Street Workington in an area of grime covered red brick terraces built not far from the steelworks at Moss Bay where Dad worked. They lived in the house behind the shop and the last time Jon had seen them he had got into trouble. It was 9 December 1960 and he was sitting in the room behind the chip shop with Father, Mother, Dad, Gill, Mam's sister Ginny, a lady called Nancy and a friend who had come in to watch the television. Mam was working in the shop serving people chips at 7.00 pm when the first ever episode of Coronation Street came on the air; she said that she was going to get rid if the telly soon because she rented it and Rediffusion was expensive. Jon looked at it for a couple of minutes but swiftly lost interest - it was grownup stuff. Instead he started doing

132

something far more engaging; almost as soon as he had arrived, his Grandfather, who doted on him, had given him an early present of a joinery set. Upon reflection it was perhaps a mistake not to give him also some scrap wood, for the devil, who finds work for idle hands, was in the room grimacing with glee and pointing out a target to Jon for the attention of his saw. Above the noise of the television Mother did not notice anything amiss and the rasping sound only reached her after a few minutes, by which time Jon had managed to saw halfway through the leg of the chair she was sitting on. That was the end of the joinery set, which he never saw again and his lugs got a good skelping. It was probably deserved on this occasion.

The family had travelled back to Thurso by train after the New Year and it was the expense of this that had persuaded Father that he must obtain a car capable of doing the long journey with ease. In December 1962, two years later, the Wolseley appeared to be the perfect choice to do the long road south in style.

At Georgemas, some miles outside town they turned down the road across the flat wide space of Causeymire. Gill was already feeling sick so Mother gave her some barley sugar to suck. Jon sipped Lucozade which had the same effect. Val was immune to travel sickness – she loved being in a car and occasionally let out her catch phrase 'Tuk-a-Tuk car' till they got tired of it and asked her to say summat else or shut up. They had to stop halfway over the moors as Jon needed a pee badly. As they turned off the Causeymire onto the A9 both older children let out the time-honoured cry; 'Are we nearly there yet?' but Father said that they would not be there for another 13 hours or so. Mother had not yet learned to drive at this point so Father, who had learned to drive in the army, was doing it all. The moor had been covered in a thick fog and the roads were narrow with passing places, so Father had not been going very fast. As they commenced the drive down the coast road Father slowed down as shadows came out of the mist on the right and hundreds and hundreds of deer began to cross the road heading for the coast on the left. Luckily most of the herd was behind the car so the delay was not long. Past the whalebone gate at Latheronwheel and on to Dunbeath, down, down, down the notorious hairpin bends and then on to the even worse hairpins at Berriedale braes they went and past one of their waymarks – a white house wall covered with antlers.

Once past Helmsdale the road ran along the coast and the terrain got better. Father negotiated through the small town and past the station. Here the road and railway ran together, the trains and the sea being on the left over a low red stone wall; the road was straight and wide so Father put his foot down and the Wolseley sped up. He was accelerating when suddenly there was a loud 'BANG' and the car was veering all over the road; he managed to avoid a head on smash with an oncoming car and brought the Wolseley to a halt finally on the small pavement to the left, and was pale and shaking at the close shave he had had with his entire family aboard. The offside front tyre had blown out completely.

Father was not happy about this but Mother and the children had to sit on the wall as he jacked up the car and fitted the spare; it did not take him long as he was very competent with his cars but not so good at choosing them.

Jon was getting desperate by now because he needed another pee. Mother was feeling rather frazzled and snapped at him that he always needed a pee but he'd have to tie a knot in it because there was nowhere to do it. As Jon whined that he could not hold it because he was going to bust, she told him to pee against the wall.

'I can't – there's too many people.'
That was true – there were quite a lot of cars going past and staring out to see what was the matter with the broken down car. Mother did not care. She said;
'I'm going to give you a new name and call you Piss instead of Jon. You will pee against that wall now or you'll feel the flat of my hand'.
He did what he had to do and cried as he did so, as many cars went past.

The humiliation of it was completed a few weeks later when two people in school told him that they'd seen him peeing against a wall near Helmsdale before Christmas.

Eventually they got going again and went on without incident. Above the town of Golspie was a huge statue on a hill and both the children wondered who it was. Father said it was the Duke of Sutherland who

134

had lived a hundred years before. When Jon asked what he had done to have a statue Father snorted and said that he had got very rich by being nasty to people. He had wanted to put sheep on his land and had to get rid of the people who lived on it – so he forced them off it. It was clear to the children that the Duke was a bad man and did not deserve a statue. On past Spinningdale where Mother, as she always did, told them that the famous actor James Robertson Justice had a house there. Before too long they were in Inverness and Father found a garage where he could get another tyre; he did not wish to continue further south without a spare.

The tyre mechanic was a dour Scot with dark blue dungarees and an army beret on his head and he changed the shredded tyre very quickly then looked at all the other wheels with a professional eye.

'They're all retreads sir – every one of them and no very good ones either. I'd advise you to change the lot or to go no faster than 50 at any time.'

Father could not afford to change all of the car tyres at once so promised that he would stay at 50 or below, so once again they were on their way.

Strangely, what was to come was foreshadowed beside the road as they left Inverness on their way South. By the road was one of the black wooden AA boxes with a white roof, and standing by it was an AA patrolman with a motorbike and sidecar. Father had an AA badge on the radiator grille of the car and as Father drove past, the AA man straightened up and saluted. Jon was much taken with this and asked why he had saluted and Father replied that all AA men saluted their members. The boy decided right away that being saluted was a good thing and he would be in the AA when he grew up.

Southwards, southwards to the Pass of Drumochter where the railway line runs alongside the road. Strange to see in this stark wilderness with snow fences on the banks beside the carriageway, a double headed steam engine pulling a passenger train heading on its way out of Inverness. The children were very disappointed when Father would not race the train because it appeared to them that their car could go a lot faster. He told them that he could not go above 50 and he was doing that, so they had to be content. Then the engine died.

Father had the bonnet up and was fiddling with it for about 30 minutes, but he could not get the thing to start again. It was nothing to do with fuel – he had done his usual request at the garage in Inverness before leaving;
'Four shots and four gallons please.'

Jo knew that the shots were something called Redex, which was supposed to make the car run better but in this case the car had broken down. In the distance was a bright red phone-box and it was downhill. Father put the car into low gear and slowly it moved down the slope and came to a halt by the box.

It was not the same AA man they had seen earlier, but he fixed the car - some wire was not working as it should and the AA man put a different one in. He also asked Father how long he had had the car and Father told him not long. The AA man thought that the engine had major problems and needed a thorough overhaul; to him it appeared clapped out and a lot of parts needed replacing. He wished Father good luck on his journey and went on his way.

Father nursed that car all the way down to Workington and there were no further incidents. Mam and Dad no longer had the fish and chip shop of two years before. They had moved, and he parked outside their house and they all went to bed. It was late and they were tired out. The next day he went to see someone called Rupey Graham who owned a garage and he went in the Wolseley and came back on foot. He announced that he had sold the Wolseley to Mr Graham, whom he apparently knew, and had bought a new car. Not a second hand car, but a new one. The cheque would have to clear and he would be picking it up after Christmas.

Mam and Dad had really done it this time – they had moved into a mansion - or what was left of one. At one time it had been a big Queen Anne House on three storeys, but it had been divided into three houses and had lost a lot of its former grandeur. As you looked at the front the house on the right was a ruin. Its roof was falling in and the windows were blank while inside the floors had fallen and were rotting with vegetation growing in there. The house on the left was run down but inhabited, with filthy windows and nets, rotting woodwork and flaking old paint. The middle bit was immaculate with painted railings stopping you falling down a gap into the cellar lights, new pebble dashing, and a small bridge running to a front door that was slightly wider than a normal house door. Inside it was beautiful for stepping through the front door it had a marble floor like a palace, dark red lincrusta up to a dado rail and old but good wallpaper up to a corniced ceiling. Along the corridor you came to broad steps running up to bedrooms and above that to what had been the servants quarters but which were now the attic. To the right of the main corridor were two rooms, back and front of a good size and filled with massive wooden furniture. An enormous redwood dresser dominated the front room, richly shining and polished; that did not protect it from Mam who, when she tired of it, chopped it up for firewood. The corridor ended in wide stairs that went down six steps onto a small landing where stood a grandfather clock and where also was a small toilet. Turn left and continue down to the cellar and back scullery, which were actually the living area of the house with a door that opened onto a concrete yard. The house was built on a hill so you entered at ground level by the front door, went downstairs and emerged down the bottom of the hill by the back door.

The downstairs room was cosy, and dominated by a table over which there was a lamp with an adaptor with an iron plugged into it for Mam was ironing when they arrived. There was no bathroom, for in these days of one bath a week, working class folk had no need of such. There was a tin bath over in the corner near the gas fire and Jon liked that. For some reason a tin bath filled from a large pot that lifted water out of a corrugated barrel with a gas ring under it, on the rug in front of the fire, was so much better than just getting into a bath like they did at home. The barrel was what Mam did her washing in, putting water in with a hose from a cold tap in the scullery, prodding the clothes up and down with a thing that looked like a metal plunger called a posser, and throwing in something called washing soda which came in white crystals.

Round the table was where the family sat for dinner – and indeed all meals. Mam was an excellent cook and a particular favourite was

Tattypot, which was a Cumbrian take on Lancashire Hotpot, which Mam used to add sage to and cook in the oven until brown and crispy on top. Liver and bacon was another, but nobody could cook belly pork like she could in a frying pan with sage and onion. Strange to say, Jon also liked her version of tripe with onions. After dinner, in the absence of a telly, there would be games on the same table. Dad was fond of dominoes and used to plant them down with an emphatic smack, and was made more interesting by a penny a game pot in the middle. Another game, played for matchsticks or pennies, was Put and Take for which Dad used a small brass spinner which he carried in his waistcoat pocket and which he said had been popular in the 1920s.

The back scullery was where the gas fire was, and there Dad used to sit rolling cigarettes of Golden Virginia Shag, and smoking them right down as far as he could, holding the stub in a holder fashioned from a paper clip, and drinking coffee made from thick condensed milk and Camp coffee which came in bottles. They used bottled coffee because Mam had taken against using instant, which did not dissolve properly when the boiling water was put on it, leaving little lumps of coffee floating on top. 'It looks like lumps of shag floating in my coffee!' She repeated this with a loud laugh.

Dad could see things that other people could not, and Jon never knew whether or not to believe him. He had been in hospital the previous year after crashing the moped he rode outside Harrington Road cemetery at 5.30 in the morning on his way to shift at the steel works where he drove a stationary steam engine working the rolling mill that made railway lines. He was found lying on the road unconscious and when he woke up and was asked how he had happened to crash his bike on a deserted road at such a time of day, he said that he had been passing the cemetery and a horse drawn hearse had come through the closed gate carrying a coffin and two men sitting up on top. The fact that he could see right through them had startled him into steering to avoid them and straight into the kerb. Of course everyone scoffed at that – as they would, but Dad had been off work for a few weeks until his concussion had healed; then he was back on morning shift.

Now he decided to do what he had always done before he bought the moped and walk. Jon's Grandfather was singular in that he liked to walk the back lonnings - the alleyways between the terraced house to get to work; perhaps this was because it did not wake his wife who was still sleeping upstairs. He let himself quietly out of the back door, crossed the clean swept yard with the mangle in the corner, and out the back gate into the lonning. Lonnings were clean and clear in those days and kept swept; it was cold, crisp and, being winter, still dark, though just getting light enough to see. Down his own lonning he went, crossed the street and into the next one. He could follow these alleys for most of his way to work. This morning, going to work he saw a figure coming towards him and realised that it was Don, a man from his own shift at work. Passing each other Dad said;

'Morning Don...'

and went on his way. 5.45am, dark and cold, is no time to linger. There was a pause for Don did not answer and Dad stopped and turned to see the other man turning to look at him. Then there came a hesitant;

'Morning Jack.'

The two men turned and continued on their respective ways. That morning, at tea break Dad mentioned that he had seen Don on his way in and asked how long it had been since he changed shifts? There was a sort of stunned silence. Then one of the other men said;

'Jack – Don died three weeks ago.'

He had dropped dead of a heart attack. Dad never took the back lonnings to work again and stayed rigidly to the streets, lit by gaslights and bright.

On this visit, their first to the new house, Dad told the children that this house was haunted. This slightly spellbound them but he smiled and told them that there was nothing to worry about. He had been going up the stairs towards the attics and he had seen someone coming down towards him. It was a lady in a long dress and a high hairstyle, quite nice looking and with small buckled shoes peeping from under the hem of her dress; the great thing about her was that he could see through her. She took no notice of Dad at all but came down towards him. He said that he flattened himself against the wall and that she passed him as if noone was there – until he, who was not worried by this at all said;

'Excuse me.'

139

She stopped and turned as if to question and looked right at him.

'I don't know who you are,' he said 'But we have just moved into this house and so that there is no misunderstanding I want you to know that you are very welcome here'.

The ghost made no reply but smiled.
'Where are you from?' asked Dad.

Once again the ghost did not speak but smiled and pointed to the wall in a westerly direction. Then she went down the stairs, into the front room, and was gone. Just over the road of High Church Street Workington was, and is a high stone wall bounding the church yard. Backing onto it inside, and less than 20 yards from the house, are high gravestones from the 18th century, and the one nearest to the house is that of Lady Anne ********* who lived in High Church Street then.

Reader, you may doubt the truth of all this but to this strange tale there is an addendum whose veracity is easily attested to. Some things you see when you are little, and you never forget them; the author has a memory dated to when he was 18 months old. Val was nearly two years old and it is to her you must turn for corroboration of the following.

During the family's stay in Workington, Mother and Father slept in the front room on the ground floor level whilst Val slept in the room next to theirs in a cot. The light in the outside passage was left on for her; just outside her room were the six steps leading down to the landing where stood the Grandfather clock.

Dad was puzzled by the clock, because although he made sure it was wound up and correct every night when he went to bed, since the arrival of his guests it had been stopping every night. He was thinking of having it taken apart and overhauled. Then one morning, over breakfast, he could not understand it at all – the clock had not stopped. Both Father and Mother expressed surprise but could not account for it. Then Dad looked at Val who had a guilty look on her face and he said gently, for he was a gentle man; 'Do you know owt about this lass?'

Gradually he got the story out of her for Dad was very good with children and he pieced things together.

The grandfather clock had a loud tick. Worse, it chimed the hour, the half hour, the quarter hour. This of course kept a certain toddler awake. So each night, when all was still and quiet, Miss Irritated of Thurso, was toddling out of her room, down six steps and was opening the door of the Grandfather clock as she has seen Dad do. Then she reached in and stopped the pendulum whilst declaiming at it;

'Shut up!'

This was fine – the mystery of the stopping clock was solved. The next development however gave the assembly much pause for thought.

'Why did you not stop it last night?' asked Dad.
'Cos the lady told me not to,' came the reply.
What lady?

Actually the lady had not spoken at all. Val had toddled out of her room and gone down to stop the clock and in fact did so. Then she turned around and the lady was standing there looking at her. To Val the fact that you could see through this lady did not signify – she was a grown-up and you did what grown-ups said. The lady was apparently smiling broadly, leaned down to look at Val and wagged her finger at her in a reproving manner. Val looked at her and understood, nodded vigorously, turned and started the pendulum swinging again. The lady then smiled and went off upstairs.

Such things are made of stuff that you do not forget. Val would remember this as clear as a bell and if you, reader, wish to know if the above is true, then you will find that she will swear to it on any number of bibles you wish to produce – and even more if you buy her a decent beer - no rubbish mind you!

Jon loved Workington for the ambience of it but not the atmosphere. As you approached the town you could smell heavy industry quite literally for a black and perpetual cloud hung over the entire area. The smell was heavy like spent matches and sulphur and after a short time, if you

141

blew your nose, your handkerchief would be black – lots of people had bronchial troubles. Yet there was something about it in its old buildings, its salty and straight talking folk who looked right at you and said what they thought and the aura of Victorian prosperity that pervaded it. It was surrounded by working coalmines, and a massive steel plant from which, at night when the Bessemers blew great glares flung up into the night sky. For an emblem of the town though you would have to choose Siddick just on the northern edge, for Siddick was a sight to see. Over the years a huge spoil heap had grown up from the coal mine there, looming large at heaven knows what height, and flat on the top - but Siddick was alight. Spontaneous combustion in the coal spoil and dust had set the heap on fire in a massive flame that burned for years. Father said that three men had gone for a walk over it for a dare and fallen through into fiery hell, never to be seen again. It may or may not be true, but Siddick at night could be seen for miles with blue, red, green flames flickering lambent over the entire surface of the heap, unquenchable, unremitting and ongoing – and imperceptibly, year on year, the spoil heap burned lower whilst the whole area smelled of coal smoke.

On the street corners and in the streets and outside pubs were men in flat caps, waistcoats, and dark jackets, almost like a uniform. To Jon they looked old – 70 he would have said, many with shrunken jaws that told of no teeth. In fact many of these men, old before their time, were no more than 40. The area and the work did this to them and turned their wives into flowery aproned matriarchs gossiping shrilly as they holystoned the front steps in the mornings.

Jon loved it when it rained because most of the centre of Workington was lit by gaslights and the rain fell onto the hot canopies over the old lights and sent steam up into the air, which looked like something back in time from another age. Strangely he also liked to wander down to the Marsh side where there were large freight yards and numerous steam trains, lending the station a curious puddingy smell which you got nowhere else wafting over the goods yard where the yellow three wheeled parcel floats waited to take their loads round the town when the goods came in. A more different place to clean and washed Thurso would be harder to imagine.

142

High Church Street stood on a bank looking down on Low Church Street and once had neighbours - long demolished. To one side of it the bank turned to a low cliff in which could be seen chimneys and brickwork from long gone houses. Indeed in the back scullery was a doorway, which led under the hill into a room without windows, which was under the ground. It was here that Dad had caught his pet spider Albert whom he kept in a matchbox with little airholes, in his waistcoat pocket. Jon had never seen anyone with a pet spider before, even less a big black one that filled half a Swan Vesta box. Dad had a party trick which he demonstrated more than once, but which Jon was never able to replicate – he could snatch flies out of the air and would then pull their wings off and put them into the box for Albert.

Coming out of the main door of the house it was a different matter. Just across the road was a narrow road between the high churchyard wall and a beautiful row of bay fronted houses called Dora Crescent which were everything that 19th century terraced houses should be. It was like something out of a picture book with cobbles on the street and Jon loved to run along it if Mam sent him on errands. It opened out into a large square called Falcon Place, but Mam and everyone around there called it Hagg Hill. Once, sent for a pint of milk from the shop, Jon found a bunch of Teddy Boys sitting on a low wall just as the crescent opened out. They were in their teens and trying to look cool, slicking their hair back with Brylcreem – or the poor man's alternative which was chip fat - and seeing Jon running towards them one stuck his leg out to trip him up. Without breaking stride Jon flew through the air shouting 'Nyah!' and ran right on with utter disdain. They didn't have a hope. He went back round the other way with the milk though when he returned.

Mam seemed to be rather sharp with a lot of people but with Jon she was wonderful and she doted on him as he on her at this time. A small birdlike woman with bright eyes and an acquisitive nature, she filled her house with 'bargains' from Lancasters the local saleroom. The houses that she and Dad lived in were all in her name for whatever reason and she was quite tempestuous in her dealings with them. They had once lived in a nice suburb of Workington called Seaton, but Dad had come home one day from work to be told that she had sold the house and was buying a fish and chip shop because she wanted to make money and that was the best way to do it. After a couple of years she tired of that, got

143

herself a job at High Duty Alloys in Distington in the canteen, and sold the chip shop. Perhaps living in a mansion was too much of a temptation for her but it did look grand.

In the days before Christmas she told Jon to get on his jacket because he was coming with her to meet his Great Grandmother, her mother, who was a very old lady called Mrs Bell. Off they trotted. It was quite a long walk but Mam could shift fast for a small woman and they walked a long way out towards Salterbeck. She did not seem puffed out at all and eventually they came to a row of modern terraced houses up a bank, each with a path leading neatly upwards, and it was up one of these that Mam strode and knocked on the door. It was opened by a very old lady indeed, with white hair, and Mam introduced Jon to 'Mrs Bell'. To Mam her mother was always spoken of with that allocution.

There was tea and there was cake in the front sitting room, which was warm and heated by a gas fire. Mrs Bell did not go upstairs any more for she could not walk very well but slept in the same room on a bed at the back. Much of the time she spent in the front room and had a television, which, she thought was wonderful, and she had not had it very long. It was a curious thing to Jon that Mrs Bell evidently thought that the people in the television could see her as she could them; it was on when they entered the room and Mrs Bell kept it on for a few minutes to listen to the weather man who was apparently a local man called Jack Armstrong and came from Bransty just a few miles down the road. The old lady chatted to the weatherman and made exclamations as he unfolded what weather was on the way. She did not like the forecast at all. It seemed that the south of England was to be covered in snow. Eventually he finished and said goodbye – and Mrs Bell also said Goodbye to him. Then she switched the television off and Mam started to speak to her.
'Shhh – you have to wait for the dot to go away – they can still see you.'

Finally the white dot in the centre of the television screen faded away and it was safe to talk.

Mrs Bell assured Jon that she always switched it off at night after the national anthem and waited till the little dot faded because they could see out until it had gone; 'And I don't want them to see me in my smalls!'

She and Mam evidently found this hilarious for they both laughed. Eventually they left and Mam said; 'We'll just swing round by your Uncle Tommy's.'
As they walked down the road back towards town Mam gestured –
'Barwise used to live there…. Ommy lives there…'

It was plain to Jon that he had a lot of family members living in the area who were complete strangers to him and he wondered if he would ever meet them.

Jon had met uncle Tommy before; he was a coal miner and worked at Lowca pit over near Harrington as a shot firer. Lowca was a big pit with a huge flat topped spoil heap running down almost to the edge of the sea; it did not quite reach the water because the coastal railway ran between the heap and the waves. Father had said that three foolish lads had been playing on the track there when he was Jon's age and the train came and turned them into three little heaps of mincemeat. Jon had been along there with Mother when he was five and she got very excited pointing at a fin in the water which they could see out of the railway carriage and said it was a dolphin, but Jon thought it much more exciting to think it was a shark with big teeth. Uncle Tommy met them as Mam came to the door of the house and a girl with straight dark hair who was older than Jon and looked very sophisticated was just leaving.

'Say hello to your cousin Ruth,' said Mam.
'Hello,' said Jon somewhat shyly – he was not used to talking to older girls.
'Hello,' said Ruth who had more important things on her mind than small boys and went on her way.

There was another cousin there called Jane but she was a girl and smaller than Jon. She wore a light dress and had straight hair and a fringe and seemed not to have any more time for boys than Jon had for girls. After saying hello, with a look that Jon thought was dislike she went off to do what she wanted and left Tommy and Mam to chat. Jon was given a drink of squash and a piece of lemon tart. Uncle Tommy

145

said he had made the pastry himself but had added the lemon topping after and next time he was going to put it on before putting it in the oven. It was quite nice all the same and when Jon saw Mother next he asked her if she would make a lemon tart. Eventually they left Tommy and went back to Church Street Mam remarking on the way that Tommy had grown a beard and she preferred him without it but it was his business.

Over the next few days before Christmas there were other visits – to Mam's sister Ginny who was older than Mam and had an eye with a large squint which Jon found fascinating, and then to 55 Devonshire Street where lived Dad's brother Joe who was quite tall and spare, with a bad chest. Mam found that someone else was visiting at the same time whose name was Nancy so they did not stay long – Mam and Nancy appeared not to get on very well. This was just as well for Mam wished to do some shopping down Finkle Street and visited her favourite shops - Porky Haig's butchers, Home and Colonial Stores and Liptons. Jon's reward came in the shape of a visit to Ben Shaw's, which was, in theory, a music shop, but in practice sold a lot of fascinating things in the toy line. He had already purchased a gyroscope there on a previous visit but now they went in and he saw something to spend his money on, inspired by his uncle Derek. Derek was Father's younger brother and was now in his late teens and still living at home – his ultimate plan was to join the Royal Air Force. A couple of days before, Derek had ridden into the yard on his bike, which he had not had for long; it was a splendid one and he had saved up for it a long time and it was his pride and joy. He then commenced to practice in the downstairs room on an accordion, which he had learned to play. To Jon this uncle seemed to be something of a genius because he could not only play the accordion but brass as well and had a cornet and a tuba. Being a good uncle he let Jon have a blow but he could not get a peep out of it. When Derek told him to blow as if doing a raspberry he did get a sort of moan from the instrument but it was evident that he did not have the 'mouth' for it. Derek then said;

'Look kid – if you want to play a musical instrument then you might try a mouth organ- all you have to do is suck and blow.'

He also presented Jon with a very small Diana air rifle that fired pellets and darts, which he said he did not need any more and Jon would enjoy having it – which he certainly did.

In Ben Shaw's Jon bought himself a mouth organ and found that sure enough, all you had to do was suck and blow. He might have driven people mad, but there was a persistent and obsessive side to him which would not give up and within a very few days he was beyond doing scales and was playing a slow version of John Peel – what other tune could it possibly be for a Cumbrian?

On another expedition Mam took Jon through Curwen Park, in which there was a large ruin and she said that the last member of the Curwen family to live there had been a lady who died in the 1920s and her will had left the hall to the town. The council, according to Mam had let it go to rack and ruin and had not used it for the public as the will had said. It was apparently very beautiful inside, but the roof had rotted and fallen in, the windows were broken by vandals, and nature was taking it over. It was, said Mam; 'Scandalous! Scandalous!'

This was one of her favourite words; then she told the story of Sir Henry Curwen who was a wicked man who died hundreds of years before. He had been so rotten that eventually his enemies broke into the Hall one night and murdered him. They had dragged him from his bedroom down the stone staircase, his head bumping on every step and by the time he got to the bottom his head had fallen off. Jon must never go near the Hall at night as everybody round here knew because if you were there at night you might hear a bump, bump, bump, as a ghostly head came down the stairs - but never be in the park as it grew dark. Sir Henry, now known as 'Headless Harry' rode through the park every night, careering furiously on a black horse, a man all in black with no head – and he would never rest until he had found it. If you saw him he would hunt you and lash you across the face with his whip scarring you for life and ride off laughing a demonic screech. Mam seemed to relish this last bit, and as it was getting dark Jon was glad to get out of the park gate. He did ask where the murderers had put the head, and Mam said they had thrown it down the well so he resolved that if ever Headless Harry cornered him then he would tell him where his head was and then he would not be whipped across the face.

147

It was about then that Dad put Jon off black grapes, indeed all grapes, as he had been eating rather a lot of them. After watching him polish off yet another bunch Dad looked at him with a sort of slantendicular look that he had and said;

'Did you enjoy them?'
'Yes I did!'
'Good – I'm glad. Them's the best black grapes you can get in Workington.'
Jon's curiosity was aroused and he said;
'Where do they come from?'
His grandfather gave a strange half smile and said;
'From the market. We buy them from a fella that has a greenhouse up Finkle Street.'
'I thought grapes couldn't grow in this country.'
'Oh they can if you have a greenhouse and his is right up against the wall of the Methodist churchyard'.
There was a pause to let this sink in and then Dad continued;
'Yis – the roots of the vines must go down under the wall into the churchyard. Plenty of fertiliser there.'

Dad, no doubt, had a rather macabre sense of humour, and for sure there were enough black grapes thereafter for everyone else in the house, because Jon never ate them again. Ever.

Mam decided that she would take Jon on a mission on Christmas Day. Dinner in her house was after 2 but Mam, who worked in a canteen and took cooking in her stride, had everything ready and sorted long before then. It was about 12 noon when she put a roast dinner on a plate and under a tin lid and set off with it across about half a mile of terraces with Jon beside her. They were going to give the dinner to Harry because otherwise he would not get a Christmas dinner. It was never clear quite who Harry was but Father said he was a dustman who used to live near the fish and chip shop who kept hens in his back yard and used to sell Mam eggs. She had taken it upon herself to look after him, saying that he did not have two pennies to rub together and needed looking after, the poor man. He was also a rag and bone man who had a horse that farted a lot, a yard at the end of a row of terraces, and a house

148

in the middle of the terrace. Mam did not bother knocking at the door but went in shouting; 'Harry- I've got your dinner.'

Jon had never been in a house remotely like it, for it was full. Mostly it appeared to be newspapers and magazines piled high up to the ceiling with piles of books, stacked furniture and everything you could possibly think of that would fill space. There were bronzes, spelter figures, sets of horns, pewter mugs, brass figures of all descriptions and junk of all sorts. Father and Mother used to laugh themselves silly at a programme on the BBC called Steptoe and Son, which showed a rag and bone man's house and yard, but compared to Harry, in clutter and junk they were rank amateurs. Mam threaded her way through a maze of newspapers and eventually found the man she was seeking smoking in what may have been the kitchen to judge from the presence of a sink, but you could see nothing else for piles of stuff. He was small, with a tanned and leathery face from being much outdoors, dressed in old trousers, jacket, and a battered trilby perched on his head, which he never took off. Never. She gave him his Christmas dinner, wished him a Merry Christmas and talked for a while and then they were gone back to Church Street for their own dinner. In truth, he did not need her attentions for when he died in 1971 his will actually got into the papers because he left a very large amount of cash indeed – but not a penny to Mam who had been bringing him food and company for decades. It all went to a horses' home where the farting horse ended his days happily. Mam must have spit feathers.

On 27 December Father went off to see Rupey Graham and came back with a white Morris Mini Minor. This caused great excitement because although the family had seen them on the television, they had never seen one live. The seats were made of a type of plastic fabric and it all smelled wonderfully new. Mother wondered at the size of it and if they could all get in, but Father laughed and said he had already considered that. It had two doors, and Father leaned his seat forward and told Jon and Gill to get in, then lifted Val in between them. There was plenty of room. Mother sat in the passenger seat and was quite satisfied with it. Father said that he had had quite enough of second hand junk and he was glad to have a new car at last.

It was when Father was outside looking under the bonnet of the new car, checking oil, screenwash and so on, that Mother was outside chatting to him when a woman came out of the run down house next door and stopped suddenly and said Mother's name.
'Edie!' said Mother. 'What are you doing here?'

Both women were delighted to see each other as they had been at school together in the late 1940s. Edie was living next door to Mam with her husband, a man much older than her and they had one child. Suddenly there was a banging at the window.

'Don't talk to her! She's no better than she should be!' shouted Mam.

Edie's face fell – she and Mam had not got on from the moment Mam had moved in to Church Street. It appeared that Edie had been pregnant when she got married and the neighbours, who loved to gossip, had told Mam. Mother said to her;

'Ah take no notice of her - she takes tich at owt,' and carried on chatting whilst Mam banged on the window shouting, but eventually she gave up.

Mother and Mam did not get on well, and were like two Kilkenny cats as Mother described their relationship. She was glad to carry on her chat as long as she wished and Mam could not do much about it. This made what Mother found on the following day entirely predictable in a way that it would not have been had Mother been a shrinking violet or had got on with her Mother-in-law.

Father used to pay Mam when the family visited and he paid her what she asked which was £8. This was a considerable amount of money but on 28 December Mother went into the room she was staying in and found Mam going through Father's pockets. The cases were open and had clearly been examined already. When she asked what the older woman was doing she was told that Father had not given her enough money and that she needed more. Mother replied that he did not have any left, and Mam said that he was well off because he had just bought a new car. Mother said that Father had paid Mam exactly what she had asked for, and had bought his car and that they had hardly anything left in the bank. When Mam said well she had to have more money to feed them all, Mother said well we have none so we'll leave in the morning.

Father had been out testing his new car and when he came back Mother told him what had happened and he agreed that they had to go. There was no use arguing with Mam on money – they were guests in her house and if the choice was between giving her the few pounds they had to get home, or going home, then they would go home. Father went to Lloyds Bank and drew out all the money he had left. It was more than enough to get home and pay their bills until the next pay went in, but it was a good job that he had it with him.

Mam had form for this sort of behaviour and it was probably because the family had come through a period of being seriously poor and they expected to share things. None of her children's stuff was safe because she felt quite free to remove it from where they put it and present it to one of the others – or to other people. Father said that he had a knife when he was a kid that he liked and he left it in his room, but when he came home from school it was gone and she had given it to Tommy who thought she had bought it for him. Father let his brother keep it, but when he started work he was quite used to his mother going into his room and looking through his pockets for cash. Father's sister Doreen was very brainy and when she finished school a few years before she had 10 grade A's for her GCEs. That secured her an offer of a place at the local Grammar School and she did well, gaining A' levels and an offer of a place at university. Mam would not let her daughter take it up. It was time that she earned her living and brought in some money. Mam had contacts at the local hospital and Doreen started work as a student nurse, sweeping the floors of the wards as they did then, the very next week. This was a great shame according to Father because Doreen wanted to be a doctor, and would have been, since she was the brainy one of the family. Cash was important, it was in short supply, and Mam, who regarded herself as head of the family, took to herself the right to manage it all. The lord of the funds would redistribute all cash, possessions and appurtenances at her complete discretion.

Jon heard later that Derek did indeed join the RAF, but when he came back on his first leave and went to get his bike, it was not where he had left it – Mam had sold it.

Next morning, 29 December and very early they said their farewells; the Mini fully loaded and the small boot packed full, set off up the road and headed for the Scottish border. By the time they got to Gretna the first flakes of snow began to fall.

Winter

Before the family set off north they had heard the news that the South of England had been hit by a massive fall of snow. Living in the Far North they were not particularly worried by this because snow was normal as far as they were concerned. There had been snow during every winter that they lived in Thurso. Reports of 20-foot snowdrifts in Kent seemed far away when Workington, though very cold, was snow free. North of Gretna the snow began to fall thick and fast but Father set the wipers going and the Mini ploughed on at a steady speed. Scotland was used to snow, the roads had been gritted and there were snowploughs out. Father was careful though, and so were most people. It was not dark exactly but the sky was heavy and mother said that there was a lot more snow up there. The road was at first slushy, but as the hours went by and they got further north the quality of it changed and a skin of hard snow began to form over the surface, so the Mini slowed down to 40, but still went on steadily as did everyone else. Between Crieff and Perth a large saloon car evidently felt that the traffic was not going fast enough and passed the line doing well in excess of 60mph.

'Bloody fool!' said Father; 'He's going to cause an accident.'

It was a two-tone green Simca and Father said it was a flashy car and too expensive for him and the driver had a small willy. That made Mother laugh but Jon could not see the connection between driving fast and having a small willy. Jon thought of God as a big old man with long hair, a long white beard and white robes sitting up on a cloud looking rather cross while watching what people were doing, and on this day he was indeed looking down and heard what Father had said. Just outside Perth the traffic slowed down, though it kept going, because there was a two-tone green Simca on its roof just up a shallow bank off the road. It must have been a tough car because the roof had not caved in and the doors were open with a dazed looking man and woman standing beside it. Jon often wished for a big foot to come down out of the sky and squish wrong doers but this day he knew that if there was not a god then there was indeed Justice, and that if Father said there would be an accident then there would be one! The police had just arrived and noone was hurt; was it unseemly that, as he drove on to Perth, Father laughed and laughed and laughed?

Until Perth progress had been quite good and Father said they would have a late lunch at Dunkeld which was good as they had been moving constantly since Workington, but there was no doubt that the snow was getting thicker and the nearer you get towards Dunkeld the closer the road gets to the Highlands. The road was only open because the ploughs were out and working wonders. The southern approach to Dunkeld was through a canyon with almost sheer sides because the snow had been carved through and ten-foot walls of snow towered above the car. Father was worried now;

'If it carries on like this we might not get home today,' he said.

Lunch consisted of sandwiches and coffee from the flask and a quick visit to the toilet where the car was refuelled and the family only stayed 15 minutes because the day was melting away and if there was a hard frost or snow then they might not be able to go further. Miraculously, north of Dunkeld and Pitlochry the road stayed open and good progress was made. It was not until they came to the pass of Drumochter where the road goes high that any trouble began. The Mini travelled round a bend and the width of the pass stretching up was in front of them and a line of cars. At the side of the road, half buried in snow there were many cars that had been abandoned but this line was moving very slowly like troops following a tank into battle. At the front of the queue was a snowplough and behind it a gritter lorry. Following them was a truck full of men and they meant business; this was Scotland in the winter and the Scots are a hardy people who will not be stopped by a few feet of snow. This road was going to stay open.

The convoy crawled northwards as the snowplough pushed the drifts off the side of the road and the miles went slowly by. Twice the snowplough found drifts that were too much for it and when that happened a flood of men jumped off the truck and attacked the drift shovelling snow to the side until the plough could get through, working like heroes, and Jon saw, with awe, that they all had bare hands. Eventually towards the top of the pass they met a team coming the other way which meant that the entire road was open, clear and gritted; for now the snow had ceased to fall. Nor was this the end of it for as the convoy moved past the snowploughs that pulled over to the side, a

154

double headed steam train, a great white plume behind it, came up from the south along the railway line beside the road, with a plough fitted on the front and at quite a rate shoving the snow off the track apparently with great ease. Snow in Scotland? No problem!

On then – it was still light and mid afternoon and there were still hours to go to reach home. Down the other side of Drumochter and along the road the ploughs had pushed the 5-foot deep snow at this point out of the way. Evidently much of the traffic in the convoy had been local for it had disappeared, Father drove on and a snow crusted sign pointed the way to Carrbridge a short way ahead. The Mini began to take a left hand bend in the road when a large van came round the bend towards them on the same side of the road. The white line was not visible under the snow and slush. The evasive action was instant – the Mini ploughed into a snowdrift on the left and the van into one on the right. The snow was soft and deep and as it happened, neither vehicle was damaged in the slightest. The Mini reversed out of the drift it was in, but the van did not. Instead the door opened and an AA man stepped out, profuse in apologies.

'I'm really sorry folks – that was my fault entirely and I was on the wrong side. I was not expecting any traffic and yours is the first car I've seen for hours. I was in a hurry because there's a lady stuck in a drift a few miles further up and I have to go help her.'

Father had a lot of time for the AA and assured the patrolman that the car was not damaged, his family were okay apart from being a bit shocked and that it was fine. Like men, they shook hands. Then the patrolman said;

'Look – you won't be able to get any further than Carrbridge because the road between there and Inverness is blocked. There's a lot of people sitting in the Carrbridge Hotel. I'll be back soon. If you go in there I will come in and tell you directly I hear that the road is open if that's a help to you.'

Father was grateful for that because although he was disappointed to be held up he knew that once the road was clear it would be a rush to get out of the place and he wanted to be at the front if possible.

155

Accordingly he drove into Carrbridge and parked, as everyone else had done, beside snowdrifts in the main street across the road from the Hotel. This was a large and impressive stone building with a type of extension on the front, which was mostly glass, painted light blue frames and with a sprung door leading into a café area. This was almost full but Mother headed for the one free table. Tea and scones it was. When they had finished there was more tea. The crowd of people sitting in there were hushed, glum and disconsolate, many wondering if they would get home that night. The floor was damp with melted snow trampled in and condensation ran down the single glazing from the heaters and the assembled warm bodies sipping tea and coffee served on trays by staff, who were rushed off their feet by the influx of people. Val and Gill simply went to sleep while Jon was bored; three hours went by.

Eventually, about 5.15 pm the AA patrolman came into the café and said quietly to Father; 'If you'd just like to follow me, sir, with your family?'

They all got up and followed him and outside he told them that the road ahead was now clear – only just and that he was going to Inverness where he lived if they would like to follow? Wouldn't they just? By now the people in the café had realised that something was happening and they were beginning to stir.

'Quick - into the car' said Father. As the Mini swung in behind the AA van there was a mad rush of people from the hotel and other places where people had taken stranded motorists in and cars began to follow them. It was getting dark so headlights were soon on. A few miles down the road Jon said that he really needed to go to the toilet, but was told that he would have to hold it because Father was not stopping. The road was slushy, gritted, and passable; the AA man stuck to a sedate speed and they approached Inverness from the south seeing the lights of the town ahead and below them. As that happened and it appeared more and more that the road going down to sea-level was clear, cars began to overtake, but Father snorted and stayed tucked in behind the AA van - no more chances for him.

At Inverness the AA man stopped and so did Father.

'I'd not advise you to go any further tonight and especially in the dark.' Father had mentioned that he lived in Thurso.

'You'd be well advised to stay in town tonight; the road ahead is bad and there's more snow forecast.'

Father thanked him again and the AA man said that it was the least he could do. They shook hands again and parted their ways. Jon said; 'Please hurry up – I need a poo bad!'

He was told that he would have to wait.

They pooled their money and Father drove into Inverness and to the Station Hotel. He parked the car and came back to tell Mother with a smile that he had enough money for a family room with breakfast for the night. Mother, Father, Gill and Val walked into the hotel, followed by Jon who was waddling. A man showed them up to their room and in they went – it was en suite and Jon gave a loud 'Waaaaaaaaa!' as he flung himself towards the door of the toilet, clawing his trousers and pants down as he did so. He did not make it and deposited a very large turd on the hotel carpet. Mother made him clear it up and clipped his ear - but not too hard for, as she told him later, he had informed them of his need and perhaps they could have found him a loo earlier if they had listened. Mother seemed to find it very funny for some reason, but Jon did not. It was kids who cacked themselves, not young men like him.

The hotel was quite plush with red wallpaper, wood panelling and heavy green covers to the beds. Dinner that night was what was left of the sandwiches, because Father did not have money to buy food, telling Mother it was a choice of petrol or food. They all slept rather well and had a good breakfast of porridge, bacon and eggs the next day and that would be it until they got home where there was food in the cupboards. At the filling station Father asked for two shots and two gallons which he said was enough to get home and told Mother that he had eight pence left in his pocket.

Snow had fallen during the night, but the journey was good down on the East coast where the roads were salted and clear with acres of virgin

157

white snow everywhere to be seen. It was however getting colder and newspaper headlines were saying that the sea had frozen over in the South of England. Father figured that the cold was heading north and that they had better get home before the big freeze arrived up here. He thought it unusual that England was colder than the Far North of Scotland, but at Alness he found that the road over Struie was closed – there would be no short cut over the moors this day. This meant the long trek round the coast through Invergordon then Tain. These, Jon was told, had been the places where the Royal Navy based its battle cruisers during the First World War and he looked out over the grim grey waves of the firth and almost seemed to see lines of huge iron ships out there with great guns. It was not a good place for the navy said Father because the men on the ships had mutinied in 1931 over pay and were led by a man called Len. Mutiny had to be explained, but Jon wondered what happened to Len after leading the navy on a strike.

North of here was clear all the way until they reached Berriedale. It had snowed here on the braes and the road had snow on it and as the Mini reached the top of the hill it had to stop as a line of cars stretched down and round the notorious hairpin bends and halfway up the other side. The cars only went halfway up because a lorry had failed to take the hairpin going up and its wheels had skidded on the snow and it was completely blocking the road in both directions. The police were handing it with assistance from the AA who were much in evidence. Just across the road from where they stopped was an AA Landrover equipped with snow chains and its driver's curiosity was evidently much piqued by the sight of the Mini. He got out of his vehicle and wandered over as father wound down his window.

'Morning sir. You'll be stuck for a wee while, but there's a tow truck coming down from Wick that should be able to clear that lorry out of the way soon. How far have you come?'

Father explained that they had been travelling from Cumberland since yesterday morning and that they were on their way home to Thurso.
'All that way in this weather in that wee carr-ie?' The capabilities of the Mini had impressed him – he had not seen one before. Providentially, as he spoke there was movement on the other side of the valley and an enormous tow truck was seen coming down the hill.

There was no problem for it to do that because the road above it had been scraped clean and gritted. Everyone got out of the cars to spectate and it actually did not take long. The truck had a crane on the back and a hook which was attached to the trapped lorry and then it simply hauled it round to the point where it should be, the driver got in and drove slowly up the steep slope to the top and on his way. There was a loud cheer from the watching crowd and then people got back into their cars; it took an hour for the Mini to get to the top on the other side as the road was still icy down into the valley floor and the police only let one car at a time make the crossing so that workmen could scrape and grit the road where the vehicles had been standing. After that it was easy and within another hour the family stood in their own house with Mother saying; 'For God's sake put the heating on!'

What Father suspected was true they had indeed been in a race against the weather and they had won it. That night it snowed like the end of the world and they woke to find three feet of snow outside. It was good to be home.

Jon's room was at the side of the house and his window was covered with a thick layer of ice and he scraped a peephole to see a world of white - and it was really cold - so cold that the warm air central heating was struggling to cope, so the convector and electric fire were also pressed into service. Walking downstairs he looked out on St Andrews Drive and saw that the snow was almost up to the windowsill, but that the road was passable for cars. It was not devoid of snow but vehicles had been along it and compressed the snow so that although it lay packed and thick, it could be driven along. After a few minutes he saw a woman in anorak and bobble hat, a bag strapped to her back, heading down the middle of the road to get her shopping on a pair of skis. That was novel.

The milkman was a stern character and he had made his round and there were two bottles on the step, but they had frozen and the cream was sticking up out of the neck with the foil lid on top and one of them had cracked with the cold. The birds had pecked at the cream on one of them and Mother cut the cream off and threw it away saying that birds carried Parrotitis and she did not want to catch it. Jon wondered if you turned into a parrot but she said it was a nasty disease and could kill

159

people so he thought it as well not to have the cream as he often did on his cereal – or in this case as ice cream.

You can do a lot with snow and Jon and Gill built a snowman on the front grass with a small carrot for a nose and two pebbles for eyes and some more for a mouth. They did ask for a hat and scarf to put on him, but Mother said she had no hat and scarf to waste on a bloody snowman so he had to stay cold. Much more amusing was what happened later when a group of adults came out to play across the road. Jon and Gill had never seen grownups playing like this - all wrapped up and throwing snowballs at each other, but the great fascination was what they did with some rulers. They used these implements to cut square lumps of snow out of the thicker drifts and then they built an igloo big enough for one of them to crawl into. It might not have been their intention but the snow house stayed there for the next three months though by that time noone was going in it. The local dogs, or at least Jon thought it was dogs, had left yellow patches up the sides and it was not a good idea to go crawling in there – there was also a white dog poo by the door. Jon never understood why some dog poo was normal colour and some was white but he stayed away from the igloo.

Fun was to be had just over the wall in the field, which sloped down. Over many years the river had shaped terraces in the side of its valley and just over the wall from the house was a slope down to a terrace, then another slope and a second terrace, then another slope to the flood plain of the river. Jon and Gill had no sledge or toboggan as posh people called them, but they did have a large tray which Mother let them use and they happily slid down onto the first terrace for much of the morning, pelted each other with snowballs and got frozen before going inside to watch the television. Everything stopped for *Top Cat*. In much the same way Mother and Father both stopped what they were doing for '*That was the week that was*' which was a funny programme about the news. Mother liked David Frost but Father preferred Millie Martin, but Jon and Gill did not like any of it and would much rather watch a western.

This was New Year's Eve, Hogmanay, so the children stayed up late except Val to whom it had no significance at all and she went to sleep. It was always the same since the television had arrived in the house. At

160

11.25 pm Andy Stewart came on the telly with his 'White Heather Club' and Jon hated his guts. Even at this tender age Jon had a strong bloody-minded streak and he wondered where this White Heather Club was and what you had to do to join it. Who were all these people dancing and reeling round the place, knowing all the steps, hooching in their tartan, poncing round in their kilts and singing these songs? Jon knew two boys who wore kilts and they were both 'orribles; the music he and his friends liked was the Tornadoes, Billy Fury, the Shadows, Spotnicks – not this stuff. And the world they inhabited was right off his mother's shortbread tin which had an unlikely looking bonnie lascie in a man's highland dress doing a Hielan dance - but Jon knew noone – even the local bygies, who dressed or acted like this. He did not like Mr Stewart at all – but Mother and Father did, so it stayed on.

This year they broke with their usual custom because they had moved house not long before and did not as yet know the neighbours.

Over at number 6, when midnight came the family immediately went out and knocked on doors. When the people inside opened they gave them a lump of coal, a piece of bread and a small poke of salt so that these things would never be lacking in that house for the coming year. If they did not first foot the neighbours then the neighbours would first foot them and it was the custom to invite folk in for a drop of something and a bit of Black Bun. This was a thick rich fruitcake covered in pastry and every housewife in the street took special care over the quality of it and this very much included Mother. If you came to Jon's house you would not only get black bun and a drink but be offered a plate of crackers with a tub of rum butter, a Cumbrian delicacy over which Mother's elbow always slipped when she was pouring the spirit, or so she said. She did the same with sherry in a trifle.

This custom seemed to be much on the decline with the spread of television and especially for Jon's family as their old friends were a cold walk away on the other side of the river. It was cold outside, and a very hard frost took hold, penetrating deep into men's souls and brains; far easier to stay at home, give Jon and Gill a thimble of sherry each at midnight and toast 1963, the New Year, then off to bed.

The snow covered the valley when they woke up. Jon, being slow, did not immediately take that in. The snow covered the valley – including the river. The family took a walk down through the snow to Thurso Bridge and found that the river was covered in a sheet of ice and in the intense cold it was getting thicker. The town was passable though because of the power station. Just because Mother Nature had decided to drop a wee bit snow was no reason for the power station to change its ways. The road from Thurso to Dounreay was kept clear at all times during the next few months, the roads gritted and salted so that people could get to work. This included Father but after he returned to work he was not there for long because he contracted his second bout of pneumonia. Once again he was in bed for a fortnight with the doctor visiting, an electric fire in the room and Mother being over-worked looking after kids and a sick man and doing almost a daily shop while taking Gill to school for now she was at the West Public.

School was great in the snow. The snowball fights every break and lunch were on epic proportions and the supply of ammunition limitless. Wars were fought, campaigns were conducted, generals made and victories won. Slides were everywhere – the teachers did not mind and indeed some of the younger ones had a go themselves. The town was open - nothing closed because of the weather and everyone went about their business huddled up in woollens and Jon favoured a balaclava as did many boys. Not only did it keep you toasty warm, but it gave a lot of protection from ambush when people jumped out and hurled snowballs at you. Jon was doubly protected for he had one of those strokes of genius that people of his age sometimes do, by putting two and two together and making five. In the frigid air of his bedroom he had decided one morning not to take his pyjamas off but to go to school with them on under his day clothes. He was certainly very warm and some of his friends thought it a good idea and they would do it themselves. Mrs Gunn probably spotted it because she remarked wryly on his nice stripey shirt that she could see under his pullover, but this could not go on. It is true that he was beginning to smell a bit gamey after three days of doing this, but then Mother grabbed him as he came in the door that evening;

'I thought so. You dirty little beast. Get them off now and they're going in the wash.'

162

Then she clipped his ear hard; that was the end of the great pyjama venture.

At the mouth of Jon's estate of Mount Vernon, every morning there was a double decker bus which took children down into town, across the bridge and out along to school. This meant that Jon's school life became less painful because the bus was always on time so he did not have to face Mr Anderson and his tawse every day. That only happened now if he missed the bus. On the way home it was a different matter – he preferred to walk back because you could do things like go into town or mess about near the river. Jon liked coming back home by following the river upstream to where there was an old iron girder foot bridge painted green that crossed just below a weir. From here, if you were determined, you could clamber up the terraces in the field where he knew he was not supposed to trespass, climb the slab fence in front of his house and be right home. It would be easier simply to walk across the river, which was by now covered in a glacier of ice two feet thick but for now he did not. He had been strictly forbidden to do this by great threats. Father had told him that the ice on the river was thin and that people fell through ice sometimes into water and drowned because they could not get back up through it. Then they became food for fishes – did Jon wish to be food for fishes? He did not so agreed to stay off the ice. If he did go on the ice then Father said he would box his ears for him. It did not matter that Jon said that the ice was really thick and that loads of other kids were walking over it – there was to be no variance to this rule and all his attempts at persuasion failed.

Rules is rules – and not getting caught is another. Jon figured that the ice was thick and there was no danger at all. He also figured that if you went part way along the river towards the footbridge then sooner or later you could not be seen from his front window so for several weeks he was merrily crossing the ice and his parents were none the wiser. In March 1963 the freeze continued almost worse than ever after heavy falls of snow in February which covered the whole country in what they said was the worst winter for 200 years. By this time Jon had friends on the estate, of which more later, but he was coming home with them and had been into town and they were about to go over the bridge. Somebody suggested that they cross instead, just upstream of the bridge where the ice was flat and slidey - indeed there were some kids sliding

163

on it already. True it could be seen from Jon's house way up on the hill, but distance would surely give him invisibility; onto the ice he went.

They had been some time there when Jon felt the ice move slightly - as did they all.

'What's happening?'
A man leaned over the bridge and shouted at them; 'Hey you kids – get off there – the tide's coming in.'

So it was – and some of the quicker boys ran over onto the Eastern shore and onto the land, turning to shout at those left on the ice to get off. Most did and finally there was only one left, Jon, who saw no reason to hurry and was strolling over when there was an almighty 'CRACK'. It was an extraordinarily loud noise and it echoed up the valley accompanied by a loud tearing sound. The tide was lifting the ice up and tearing its hold on the bank and it began to break up into floes. Jon was worried now – evidently there was a need to hurry as a gap of about a foot had opened up between the edge of the ice and the shore. He now ran over to the gap and did not like the look of the dark cold water which the thought he might fall into and looked rather deep. However, he had help in the shape of a small cloud of boys shouting;

'C'mon Jon – c'mon bygie– jump!'

So he stepped back and took a little run and jumped. The shore was icy and he started to slip back but willing hands caught him and dragged him up.

Ah well. No harm done. Until he got home, and found that Mother had got Father's binoculars out and had been watching the whole thing from the main bedroom window. Shouted at. Little sod. Fish food. Wait till your Father gets home. Clipped ears. Repeated after 6 when Father got home.

Yes, yes – Jon has been here before, but all the parents he knew were like this except Susie's who did not believe in it, and some were far, far worse.

164

The thaw set in during March and the river was soon thick with chunks of ice floating downstream. Thurso beach, which had been covered with a thick crust of Arctic like ice formed from spray and tide and foam was now sand again. The compression and pressure caused by the tide lifting the sheet on the river had created great forces and somehow some huge lumps had ended up on the path beside the river, a few feet about the water. It's a good job that noone was around when they landed. A few days after the thaw Mother was walking there with Val in a pushchair, talking to one of her friends and Jon trotting out in front when she saw the ice. She turned and said to her pal;

'Well if only I'd known it was that thick I'd have gone on it myself.'

Jon's mind was a turmoil of vindication, feelings of injustice, indignation that he had not been listened to - and If onlys. Life is full of if onlys.

It was at this time that Mother decided she was going to smarten Jon up a bit and he was going to look like a proper schoolboy instead of a tramp. He had been wearing that snotty old balaclava for too long – so it disappeared and she presented him with a school cap and a raincoat. Jon's school had no uniform, but he had had a cap before. He hated it for the look of it and the fact that any time he wore it, it got snatched off his head and chucked round the playground. At some point it had disappeared, he knew not where, but now Mother had bought another. He did not want it.

'You will wear it – and if you lose if you know what'll happen – I'll skelp your lugs for you'.

He wore the cap on the first day until he was out of sight and then into the leather satchel it went. After school he walked out capless and looked round town for a while – then walked towards home over the bridge putting it on now as the breeze hit him. It was a raw day and a hard wind was blowing off the land towards the sea bringing a mix of thin rain and sleet that coated a frigid harl on the stonework. He tugged his new cap down and was glad of the raincoat. It was when he was two thirds of the way over, going across the arch of the millstream that the great gust came and swirled the new cap off his head and down into the dark racing water. He could only watch with feelings of panic and helplessness as it disappeared bobbing in the waves, down the river towards the sea. That day he did not wish to go home but had to and eventually let himself in. He told her straight away what had happened, but to his great surprise she accepted it and nothing else happened. Perhaps it is that there are situations where the truth is writ so plain on a face, or in the aura surrounding a person, that there is actually no doubt in the mind of the person they speak to. From this time on he went hatless, but it was preferable to the cap – and infinitely more so to skelped lugs.

It was the school bus and his own character (which was sometimes akin to a feather pillow in that it took the imprint of the last head that lay upon it) that got him into the biggest trouble since moving onto Mount Vernon. Some of the older lads did not take the bus straight to school but hopped off the platform at the corner of the Post Office, then walked up to school along Sinclair Street, this allowing them to stock up on chocolate and sweets before they started the day. Jon saw this method of dismounting the moving bus as quite cool, so he decided to do it himself and jumped off the bus as it went up the hill from the bridge, and right outside the cinema. It was Aunty Joan who happened to be passing who told Mother all about it. According to her the bus 'was still doing between 20 and 25 mph when your lad jumped off it, and he fell onto both knees, tore the right trouser leg completely open and a smaller rip in the other; this was before he ended up sprawling in the gutter. That's why he had a gash on the right knee, tied up with his hanky and a blood stain on the left because there was nothing to staunch the cut with.' After Mother had finished shouting about him being lucky not to break his bloody neck, ruining his good school trousers, being a total idiot, and wait till his Father heard about this, she clipped his ear and sent him to his room.

Father did not smack him, but stopped his pocket money for several weeks to go towards a new pair of trousers, merely contenting himself by asking if Jon was thick? Jon did not think he was but evidently Father would not be satisfied with a lesser answer, so he somewhat sulkily had to admit that he was.

Sometimes we have to placate angry spirits, especially patriarchal ones, with a sacrifice of our own dignity. It is never an enriching experience, but always humiliating, however much it may be deserved.

Winter had one more kick left. By March Father was back at work though plainly not feeling at his best and he had to go away on business. What it was he did not say and Jon and Gill were not to find out for some months. It was still cold, but it was March, the thaw was well under way and the roads were clear so he decided that he would go south by car and would be back in four days; off he set in the Mini to go wherever he had to go. On the evening that he was due home he did not arrive and since he was not on call at the power station any more they had not fitted a phone line into the new house. Mother was getting more and more worried, but she sent Jon and Gill to bed at their normal time. Val had been asleep for ages. Father finally turned up at about 2 in the morning to her great relief, but it was not until the next day that a very thoughtful and very thankful Father told them why he was late. On the way south he had stuck to the coast road via Tain and Invergordon, but on the way north he had decided to take the shortcut from Alness over Strath Struie. He knew that there was still snow and ice about but to his pleasure Struie was open – it would save him miles and about half an hour on his way home. The road was so clear that he grew confident and incautious because the car was holding the road as normal and he had no problems. Finally he began the descent of Struie and approached the left hand bend where the road off the moor comes down to what is known as the Struie Viewpoint. Here the wind coming up the hill had created a patch of black ice and as he came to the corner the Mini spun out of control and went sideways at the edge of the drop. There is not a precipice off the road but a hill which drops away quite steeply and there is little doubt that any vehicle coming off the road with sideways momentum would roll a very long way down and that anyone in it would in all probability die. Father thought he had had his chips as the Mini went toward the edge; there was no crash barrier or wall, just the edge, and two completely random boulders. These two boulders were the exact length apart of a Morris Mini Minor and the car skidded precisely in between them, being held in between them as tight as a vice. Father opened his door and looked down. He could not get out that side, so he wiggled his way over to the passenger side and got out onto the road shaking like a leaf. It was cold and he could not hang

167

about so taking a torch from the glove box he set off down the hill and knocked at the door of the first house he came to and asked for help. Luckily they had a phone and he called the AA who did not take long – in fact he had just finished a hot sweet tea and stopped shaking when they arrived. The AA van towed the Mini out sideways for it could go neither back nor forward and the AA man whistled.

'You are a very lucky man, Sir. Someone up there is looking out for you.'

Father had to agree. The Mini was undamaged apart from two small dents in both front and rear bumper where the stone had dug in and gripped the car. He was able to get in and drive, very cautiously now, on his way. That was something he was always glad about because as he said, if you have an accident at anything the best thing to go is to go right back and do it again or you'll be afraid of it. Mother took the view thereafter that it was two boulders that stopped her from being a widow, but Father, who appeared more religious in some matters, thought it down to a higher power. He had made it home safe to his wife, which is probably rule number one for a married man on a journey, done his business successfully, and though none of the family knew it, his little trip had changed their futures for ever.

Running Wild

In the beginning of 1962 a family moved next door and Willy Foote from Kirkcaldy who was now at school with Jon though in a different class was just through the wall. Willy was much more worldly wise than Jon and they very quickly became pals. Nearby was Jack from Glasgow who you did not mess with at school because he was very good with his fists and his dad was teaching him how to box. These three were now inseparable as boys become very quickly when they do things together. At first it was all rather innocent and they engaged in the sorts of activities that boys are supposed to do. It was helped by the fact that Father and Mother had at last relented on the bike thing – it had been several years now since Jon's near miss with a car wheel so he now had a red bike with solid rod brakes that he was very proud of. For a while it got used quite a lot round the estate for racing others until it inevitably got a puncture on the back wheel and then it spent two weeks in the back of the garage. Eventually Father got round to showing Jon how to mend a puncture on a bike wheel and it was back in commission. He was unused to riding a bike after so long and did get a bit wobbly at first, notably in the lane behind his house when he fell off sideways whilst riding too slow and caught his knee on one of the metal struts holding on the back mudguards. It was sharp and gouged out a lump of flesh and skin, flicking it onto the floor. He looked at it, like a lump of clear jelly with some skin attached, but left it lying, a small piece of himself, while he went to stick plaster over the gash in his right knee which was bleeding a river down onto his sock. This was his first lasting scar.

Strange as it may seem Jon could at this time take or leave the bike because round the estate he found that he could run faster than his friends could ride their bikes. Their hinterland now included the local cemetery though it was not easy to get into because of a high wall and a hedge and railing fence down the driveway bordering the estate. Down the bottom of St Andrew's drive was a small driveway leading to a gate into the fields sloping down to the river. Through that gate was a tree; you could climb the tree, which was easy and get onto the top of the cemetery wall. From the wall you could see the top of the wings of a white stone angel on a grave backing onto the wall inside. It was easy

169

for a small boy to get down into the cemetery between the wall and the angel.

It was a place to hang out, sit, smoke an illicit fag or just look around with morbid curiosity. Jon liked the cemetery for one particular reason, which was that on all of the old graves it actually gave the jobs that each of the people had done when they were alive. If you walked round you would see a grocer, a carpenter, a ships chandler, a butcher, a baker and so on. On the day of judgment, when the graves would open to give up their dead, there would be no problem getting anything you needed for it these people took up all their old trades again then Thurso would be self sufficient and the rest of the world could mind its own business. So thought Jon. He hoped they would not be Zombies like he had seen on the telly in *The Ghost Breakers* with Bob Hope but real nice kind folk, hard working and with decent old fashioned shops like Hamish Cameron's - he would like that. Many of the graves were built on terraces one below the other and if there were doors in the bottoms of the terraces then folk could walk right out on the day of judgment – a far better arrangement surely than having to climb out all dazed and sleepy?

One day in the cemetery though Willy did something really bad. He announced that he was going to write in blood on a particular grave.

Jon's eyes widened; 'You'd better not do that!'
Willy took no notice at all and started to write on the grave with a blood red felt marker the words;
'I am a Homo.'
Jon was almost weeping by now;
'Willy – you'd better not do that!'
Willy was scornful. 'Why not?' he said.
'Cos he'll get up out of there tonight and come and get ye!'
There was a momentary pause and now it was Willy's eyes that widened – it was obvious that he had not thought of this.
'No he won't,' he said.
'Yes he will - when it's dark about 3 o clock in the morning'
'No he won't.'
'Why not – I think he will so!'
There was another pause as Willy's brain whirled, looking for a way out of this.

'I'll say the Lord's Prayer three times and leave the bible open by the bed! He won't come then!'

Well that was all right then. They left, and Willy did not write on any more graves. But he did look very tired the next day.

Jon never did ask him what a homo was – he had not the faintest idea; it was something boys called each other at school when they wanted to really insult them – or start a fight, which it invariably did, though noone knew what it was.

On another day there were three of them mooching round the cemetery in the sun and they came to the broken brown obelisk in the middle that commemorates Robert Dick.

Willy laughed and began to chant; 'Robert Dick was a prick! Robert Dick was a…..'

There was a shout from across the other side of the cemetery where a man was evidently very unhappy and angry as he was running towards them waving his fists!

'Run!'

They ran allright and Jon reached the stone angel first but had been brought up too strictly and his manners let the other two go first. Jack was having difficulty getting up. Jon helped him as the man closed the distance and just made the top of the wall as the man hit the bottom of the angel almost out of breath with the speed and reached up. He grabbed Jon's ankle just as he jumped for the tree and could not hold him. Nonetheless, his grip as it slipped was enough to upset Jon's balance and he did not make the tree branch but fell straight to the ground. On the way, automatic reflexes took over and he twisted in mid air and landed on his feet. He hit the ground with a lot of force and his muscles were not up to it; his chin came down onto his knees and his tongue was in the way of his teeth. He had minor scratches from his fall but bit a huge gash in his tongue. There was blood everywhere and that coppery-iron taste in his mouth so he dragged himself home and told Mother he had fallen over. The man had climbed to look over the wall

171

and seen a lot of blood pouring down Jon's face, and he never heard another thing about it. Salt-water mouthwash, stinging pain and watering eyes from the salt, but he was young and it healed quickly.

The reason why they were so interested in the cemetery during the first part of 1963 was because they were ghost hunting. That it was during the day had nothing to do with things – a ghost had been seen in the cemetery and they wanted to track it down. Mother told Jon the real history of the Thurso cemetery ghost months later, so it is set down here in context.

Just before the February 1963 snowfall, a lady whom we shall call Marjory, a friend of Mother's looked out of her window at 1am and saw that it was snowing very slightly. She was anxious for her cat Moody for he was not in the house; neither did he come when she called out of the door. Her husband was on shift so she was disturbing noone and she threw on a good thick white coat over her long nightdress and a pair of fashionable white wellies. It should be mentioned that Marjory was a tall blonde lady and got up in this manner she must have looked rather like the Ice Queen. She wandered round the estate in bright clear moonlight calling for her cat, to no avail, then she recalled that Moody liked to go into the cemetery – she had seen him in there and it was part of his territory. Marjory had no time for ghosts at all and absolutely no fear of any such nonsense so she walked out of the estate, up the road, down the drive and through the cemetery gate which was not locked. For 15 to 20 minutes she walked round the cemetery paths calling; 'Moooooooody! Moooooooody' in her high pitched voice, but no cat appeared.

Eventually it started to snow heavily and she decided to go back home the snow expunging her footprints. When she got there Moody was there, so her expedition was wasted and off she went to bed.

She did not know that in three out of the five houses down that end of Tormsdale and St Andrews Road she had caused great consternation. Mother got the story from a lady she knew in the house over the wall from the cemetery. A tall white figure had been seen wandering round the cemetery in the small hours and had been seen independently by several people in several houses. The poor soul was evidently tormented, wailing, and searching for something she had lost in life and would never rest until she found it. It was definitely not a human because there were no footprints in the snow and who would be in a cemetery at that time of night? The tale went round the estate like wildfire, but though people watched after that for several nights, the wandering phantom was never seen again. At least part of the reason for this was that Mother had repeated it to Marjory over coffee and she had gone pink, and red and; 'Oh dear, Oh no... it was me!'

Mother heard the tale, laughed and advised her not to say anything about it – thus was an urban legend born. After the adventure of the chase and his injured tongue, Jon lost interest in the cemetery.

The summer of '63 was wonderful. It was warm as the temperatures climbed after March, sunny and bright with a texture and flavour to the air that was full of life and vigour. It was the sort of time when it is pure joy to be young and alive and the scent on the breeze is electric. Down over the field and to the river, right by the footbridge was a deep part, dark and swirling. Not far upstream there was a weir and a place you must not go that Mother said was the Queen Mother's salmon pool. Once in the distance Jon did indeed see a small lady in a funny hat standing there fishing, but did not go any further than the old ruined cottage filled with bushes and overgrown with pink dog roses, past which was an invisible line where you'd be *arrestit by the Polis* if you went any further, so the other kids said. Between the weir and the bridge Willy considered it to be open season on fishing and it belonged to noone. He had a rod and pellets of bread and hooks, so down the three of them went and sat in turns on the summer grass among the big daisies that Mother called Marguerites, lying in the sun just gassing about all sorts of things. They didn't catch a thing and Jon by now thought that fishing was an utter waste of time.

Much better was the day that Willy came back from the chemist; he had told the chemist that he wanted some stuff for his chemistry set and he had a bag of what looked like yellow sherbet.

'What is it?' said Jon.
'Sulphur,' said Willy. 'And this is copper sulphate.' He produced another bag with a number of blue crystals in it.

173

'What you gonna do wi that?'
'Set fire to it – you'll see.'

Into an open garage on the estate they went, ten years old and totally ignorant of chemistry except that Willy knew sulphur went into fireworks. He piled the sulphur up in the middle of the garage floor and put the copper sulphate crystals onto the pile.

Jon was not sure about this and hovered by the door – he thought it might explode and was a bit scared, but Jack and Willy were in the garage when Willy pulled out some matches and held a lighted one to the pile. Immediately a dense cloud of gas flew up into the air hissing and choking. With a yell Willy jumped up and ran out of the garage, catching the door and slamming it down nearly all the way.

'Let me out ya basturt!' yelled Jack from inside the garage, choking and coughing. It's lucky for him that Jon was there for he pulled the door back up and let Jack out. Willy was already halfway up the road.

Jon and Jack looked at each other.
'What do we do now?'
Jon shut the garage door, round the edges of which clouds of smoke were pouring smelling like concentrated matches.
'Dunno – but let's get out of here in case it blows up!'
They sat on a wall up the road for a short while with Willy, perhaps 15 minutes. By the end of that time Jon said;
'The man will be home soon – we'd better open that door or we could be in trouble.'
None of them wanted to do it, but they saw the point and all three went down to the garage where they gingerly opened the door. A dense cloud of smoke rolled out which they leapt back from but there was no hissing - the sulphur fire had burned itself out. All that was left was a burned patch on the concrete floor, which they scuffed over a bit but could not remove it all. Then they sat on the wall in the sun as a few minutes later the owner of the garage turned up and drove in. He did sniff suspiciously but eventually closed the door and went home. Never mess with chemicals – they do serious stuff!

174

There was now, among the three companions, Jon, Jack and Willy a dare culture that said that you had to do what the others did or you were somehow in danger of not being part of the group - the gang. For some reason or other there existed an animosity between them and a group of other boys from across the other side of the estate. It seemed to have originated with Jack who used to throw stones at them and they of course threw them back. As he did so he used to shout;

'Tongs ya bas!'

Jon did not know what this meant and when he asked Jack he said that it was what his gang used to shout back in the Gorbals - which was good enough, so Jon and Willy shouted it too. When Jon asked why they were so much against the other kids Jack said it was because one of them had thrown a stane at his dug. Well that did it – you had to be a scoundrel to throw stones at such a nice wee white dug, so without any more questions Jon happily threw stones and made aggressive noises at the kids on the other side of the estate and they returned the compliment; battle lines existed in invisible ink across Mount Vernon.

One day they trooped out of school and dallied on the way home. Eventually they crossed the bridge and went into the milk shop in the old tollhouse to get some fruit gums, but they had none. No matter - there was a small shop on the corner across the road on Millbank Road, which did, so they were suitably refuelled with sugar. Over the road to peer in the eggs warehouse and look at all the cartons stashed there and thousands of eggs stamped with the little blue lion, then homewards up past the boating pond. By now it was past 5 o clock and the builders had gone home from the houses being put up along the Mill road as it rose to meet St Andrews Drive. Here were some small blocks of flats, which were incomplete, their frames rising to four storeys. The partially finished floors were in place and ladders connected them inside. It was a ready-made adventure playground and they could not resist it. The site was unfenced and they went in and before long they were climbing the ladders, swinging off wooden joists and Jon had a great time right up on top using a joist as a tightrope and walking swaying along it - there was only a two floor drop under him. Willy was right up on the roof and found a hammer just lying there so he took it and put it in his bag. Jon saw it and morality clicked into place;

'You shouldna steal that.'
'It's no stealing – it's nicking and that's different.'

There followed a brief discussion, which an adult might have seen in more abstract terms as a debate upon morality. Willy took the view that he had found the hammer and that it had just been left lying there. It was the same as if someone had dropped a tanner in the street and he had found it – it was his to keep. His will was much stronger than Jon's whose mental processes were those of a born again numpty so he prevailed, stuck the hammer in his bag and took it home with him.

A seed had been planted though and the notion that there was a difference between nicking and stealing took root in Jon's head, and it happened at the same time as he learned to lie. He had always been taught to be truthful and did not tell lies, but lately his thought processes had been working on the matter of what happened if you did not lie. Mrs Gunn had told her class the story of George Washington in History, and how he had cut down a cherry tree. When his father asked who had done it, George had owned up even though he thought his erse would get skelpit, but his father forgave him. Jon had thought much on this and he knew that if he owned up to such a thing he would not be forgiven and there would be pain. If Mother or Father asked him if he had done something wrong and he said he had not, then nothing happened. On the other hand, if you told the truth and admitted that you had done something, you got punished. In Jon's case this meant that the side of his head was slapped hard repeatedly as his lugs got skelped, or in worse cases he got the belt on his bottom. To cope with the last he had tried doing what the Bash Street Kids did and had once put a book down the back of his trousers, but Father spotted it and took it out before belting him.

There was a message here that was as clear as a bell and it was that if you told the truth then you got punished for being honest. Honesty did not pay.

Being slow to comprehend, it had taken Jon a long time to learn this elementary lesson, but now he had - and just in time.

A few days later Father asked him;
'I've heard that some boys were seen messing about where they're building those flats down the road. Were you with them?'
'No!' said Jon,
'I also heard that something was taken from there – stolen. Do you know anything about that?'
'No.'
Father looked doubtful but he did nothing. It worked - dishonesty had paid off and there was no sore bum and no clipped ears.

A few days later on a Saturday afternoon some time in September 1963 Jack said; 'Let's go nicking!'

Jon wondered what he meant but their latest venture, cherry knocking, was beginning to lose its flavour. You can ring so many doorbells and run off, but eventually it gets boring. He asked what Jack wanted to go nicking and he reached into his pocket and said;
'I got these this morning.'
He was holding a few brightly coloured pens, a small torch, a rubber, and a pencil sharpener. Willy said;
'I've been doing it too.'
So saying he pulled off the rubber grips from his handlebars and tipped the bike over. Out fell pens and pencils.
'You got to come bygie - if you don't you wilna be in our gang any more and you're a homo.'

He had no need to threaten because Jon was willing - it all sounded great fun - a new game. Not wanting to be left out Jon agreed, so Willy, Jack and Jon set out on their bikes to go nicking. They rode down into town and ended up in Couper Street where they leaned their bikes on a wall and went round the corner into Woolies.

Jon had not the faintest notion of how to go about this, so like Oliver watching the Artful Dodger he observed his two pals go up to counters and wait until the shop girls were not looking, then take things and put them in their pockets. Well this was easy! Two pencils quickly made their way into his coat and then Willy was motioning to leave.

This was nicking, which was like stealing but wasn't according to Willy because it was all a game. Jon had certainly enjoyed it – his heart had pounded and there had been a rush of excitement at doing something completely naughty - and he had got away with it! They must do this again.

The policeman came to the house late that afternoon and it was the sergeant with the moustache that all the kids in town feared. Jon did not see him come, being in the back garden, but Father called him through.

'Jon – this policeman says you were seen taking stuff from Woolies this morning. Is it true?'
Jon smiled a big grin and said; 'Yes.'
Father appeared rather taken aback and asked;
'Have you been stealing stuff from Woolies??'
'No.'
'But you just admitted that you took stuff from Woolies.'
'Yes – we were nicking – not stealing!'
Father and the sergeant exchanged puzzled glances and the sergeant said;
'You and two other boys were nicking stuff from Woolies. Who were they?'
'Me and Willy and Jack.'
'I know about Jack – we've met him before. Where's Willy live then?'
'Next door – he's in the garden.'
'Has he been nicking before?'
'Oh yes,' said Jon smiling because he still thought it a great game.
'Where is the stuff you nicked then?'
Jon produced the pencils and gave them to the sergeant.
'Do you know where the stuff is that Willy took?'
'Oh yes – it's really clever – he disnae want his Da to see it so he keeps it in the handlebars of his bike.'

The denouement of the piece took place in the garden where Willy's face fell as soon as he saw the sergeant. At first his father was indignant and tried to deny that Willy had done anything but the sergeant asked to see Willy's bike and it was brought. He tipped it sideways after removing the handgrips and pens and pencils fell out and Willy dissolved into tears. Willy's Father took it badly.

'My son's a thief! My son's a thief!' he kept on saying and ushered him indoors.

The Police sergeant said to Father;
'I'm going to have to ask you to bring your son down to the police station on Monday morning Sir. There will be no charges because of his age, but I am going to read him a formal warning and tell him of the consequences if he continues to behave in this way. I trust I can leave it in your hands to explain to him the meaning of the words 'stealing' and 'nicking?'

Father said that he could; they shook hands and the sergeant left.
'Upstairs,' said Father.

He took a belt out of the wardrobe and doubled it over and while he explained the meanings of the words stealing and nicking, Jon got six lashes of the strap on his bare bum. By the time it was over he knew what the words meant and decided that he was never going to 'nick' anything ever.

Jon never saw Willy again. Mr Foote's reaction was rather more than administering a belt. He resigned from his job and sold all his furniture within a week and the whole family emigrated to one of the Dominions. He had no job to go to, no home to go to, but wanted a fresh start.

In school Jon and Jack simply avoided each other, which as not hard as they were in different classes.

The formal warning took a few minutes and Jon was told that a record of it would be kept until he was 15 and then it would be destroyed.

The final straw was when Father came home one day and said that he had been talking with the man who ran the Sea Scouts down at Scrabster. Jon would be joining them in the New Year, 1964. He would be wearing uniform and learning some badly needed discipline because the man who ran the Sea Scouts was very strict indeed. Jon was made thoroughly miserable by this and he did not wish to be a sailor; he did not wish to go to sea and he particularly did not wish to be told to do by a shouting sailor whom he imagined with a large black

179

beard and a hard hand. The thought of this was to hang over him for most of the rest of term until Christmas.

As the year lengthened time hung heavy for Jon because he was grounded, allowed out to school, told to come straight back and not allowed out to associate with anyone else on the estate. It was natural that he should pass his time watching a lot of telly, but on 22 November 1963 he had to read a book because the black and white television with their only channel, the BBC, showed nothing but a revolving globe and played the Dead March with the occasional news bulletin. It seemed that President Kennedy of the United States had been shot in Dallas, Texas. This made little impression on Jon's world but he knew Kennedy was important having seen him in the news many times. Lying on his stomach beside one of the warm air vents, deep into a storybook and wishing there were cartoons on instead of this, it passed his ten year old mind by. It has to be said that at this age, there are not many who are politically conscious. For him it ended a few days later when Lee Harvey Oswald was shot dead by a man called Jack Ruby, names that were to lodge indelibly in his memory, but for reasons he could not fathom. Used to watching westerns like Sugarfoot or Bronco, he knew that if a good guy got shot then the bad guy always got his just desserts later. Jack Ruby had to be the good guy in Jon's book, but it cannot be maintained that this was a considered judgment.

It was as Christmas approached that the bombshell fell and the fact that it meant that Jon would not be joining the Sea Scouts did little to soften it. Mother and Father announced that they would all be leaving Thurso in January and moving down to live in England. The trip south that he had made earlier in the year had been to a job interview and Father, after long consideration had been offered a job in Burton upon Trent.

Jon did not wish to be English and live down South but wanted to stay in Thurso. Mother said that it meant promotion for Father, more pay and an increase in pocket money for Jon and Gill. She also said that they had to move because they were worried about Father's health. The winters here were far too cold and he had gone through two bouts of pneumonia and she was not going to end up a widow just to stay in Thurso so they were going to move and that was that. Jon could like it or lump it, but he was moving to England.

A last despairing card he played and moaned;
'But most of the English kids I saw down there had fair hair – and mine's brown! I'll be really odd down there!'

It did not faze her in the least and she said if it made him happier then she would dye his hair. He did not want that either so shut up about the hair thing.

Jon had left England when he was five and had hardly any memories at all of living down there – and certainly no friends. His education, his friends, his inclination were all Scottish, as was his accent at this time. A certain devastation took hold and his memory blotted the period out. Christmas 1963 was awful; New Year was dismal. Some furniture disappeared as Father sold it off. Next door was empty. The days rolled inevitably after New Year and Jon and Gill did not go back to school; goodbyes had been said, but the realisation that some of the people he took as part of his life as much as the blood in his veins, he would never see again, had not sunk in. One morning a large van with the name 'Hoults' on it pulled up outside and all the contents of the house and garage were loaded into it. Then as all their worldly goods trundled off down the road, heading for a storage depot somewhere down south, the family got into the Mini and drove round St Andrews Drive round through the entrance to the estate, and turned right.

Epilogue

Life is full of leavings, full of farewells and to humans this is a natural state. South to Mam's house in Workington for six weeks, south for a new life in England, a strange and foreign place which was alright for a visit when it was to grandparents - but for living in - how would that be?

The car headed for Georgemas, the morning was cold and dreich and Father turned the heater on full so the side and back windows clouded over. Jon squirmed round in his seat, wiping the glass to look back at the town shrouded in a slight drizzle and mist, buildings silhouetted in the gloom, spires poking up through. Quickly it began to disappear, and, eyes straining through bad visibility, Jon watched sadly as the last shadows disappeared and the poetry went out of his life.

Oh yes – there is poetry in life, even for those who cannot articulate it. Jon was no poet, but he knew that something had gone from him, something that he would never regain. Call it what you may – childhood, his experiences, his friends, his education, the culture that he grew up in and all that puts the colour into life was disappearing down the road. There may have been no angel guarding the way back, forbidding with a flaming sword, but Jon knew that his sins had found him and he had been cast out.

It's quite a price to pay for stealing two pencils from Woolies.

At Dunkeld going south Jon had minestrone soup for lunch – the only member of the family to do so. By the time the journey was over he was sicker than he had ever been in his life and for the next two weeks he could eat nothing solid. The weight fell away from him, he was weak, white as a sheet, and looked like a famine victim with huge blue circles under his eyes. Bed-rest, a visiting nurse every day and egg/milk whipped with a little sugar was all he could take. They said it was food poisoning.

Maybe they were right.
If your soul gets sick, then it is quite another discipline outside the realms of medicine.

182

He was young and he recovered well enough.

Inside his head, crystallised for all of his time, he carried his world - the one he grew up in, his childhood in Hyperborea. They were all there, Miss Bruce, Willy, Lennie, Miss Munro - all of them and more as they always will be to the end of things, and a picture of Thurso as it was.

And he carries knowledge of how it was, and who people were and what it was like to be in that time, that is worth the writing down. As all people do, he carries his secrets and records one here.

For those who may wish to find in their life that one moment where all is harmony and peace and you are washed with the beauty of the world like a balm for all ills, when all seems small and insignificant compared with the timeless place you are in, Jon knows where it may be found. As the sun disappears on a still quiet evening in Thurso, at the stone jetty that forms the entrance to the harbour there is a place of power. Let it be an evening when it is not too cold and look straight along past the small flashing light on a pole, and out over the darkening sea. To your left the lights of Scrabster twinkling across the bay in the twilight; to the right the gaping eyes of Thurso castle, derelict and forlorn, the rocks below. The lighthouse of Holborn Head and that of Dunnet flash intermittently. The plangent splashing of the ripples against the bottom of the quay and the swash of the waves along the beach may be heard clearly. The smell, through a rift in time may faintly echo the aura of a past fishing fleet and North Sea drifters in faded paint, with red-brown sails. If not, then the cold sharp air will feed lungs that breathe deep of its iodine seaweed tang. In the far distance can be seen the dark and disappearing isles of the North, a light also flashing there, and perhaps a great ship may be passing on its way through the Pentland Firth with stars twinkling atop her masts. They are nothing compared to the great and crusted vault of heaven above, aglow with a million or more lamps. There are many lovely places in the world and to the mind that is open to them they too can affirm life, clear away doubt and ill and set all right in a troubled mind. For Jon here was a place between Heaven and Earth, of magic, of mystery and of content, between worlds. It is worth a pilgrimage on your journey if you should pass that way.

Pytheas of Massilia in 325bc is supposed to have made a voyage to the end of the world at Thule. On his way he found the land of the Hyperboreans, so called because they live beyond the North wind. The bones of it are rock that is pre-Cambrian, the oldest of which are over 4 billion years old, dating back to the formation of the earth. In the bible of the Christians it states;

"And God made the firmament, and divided the waters which were under the firmament from the waters which were above the firmament: and it was so."

Here then is part of the elder land, of Eden, made by God at the Creation with his own hand; God's own county.

It is an elemental place of wind and rain, frost and snow, moor and sky. But there be no dragons, and the inhabitants thereof are friendly to strangers. They have no secret hidden in their land and they do not boast it to be better than anywhere else. Jon has no such reservations, and being full of years is willing to hold it among the loveliest places on the wide earth, but admits to a bias. Here, frozen in print, and wholly subjective, the reader may discern why.

J

November 2015

Made in the USA
San Bernardino, CA
07 January 2017